KU-519-134

GREEN GUIDE

Wild Flowers

OF BRITAIN AND EUROPE

GREEN GUIDE

Wild Flowers

OF BRITAIN AND EUROPE

david sutton
ILLUSTRATED BY colin emberson

SELECT
EDITIONS

This edition published in 2003 by
Selectabook Ltd.
Roundway, Devizes
Wiltshire SN10 2HT

First published in 1990 by New Holland Publishers (UK) Ltd

1 3 5 7 9 10 8 6 4 2

ISBN 1 84330 506 2

Phototypeset by AKM Associates (UK) Ltd
Reproduction by Scantrans Pte Ltd
Printed and bound in Singapore by
Kyodo Printing Co (Singapore) Pte Ltd

Contents

Introduction

This guide covers 150 species of wild flowers most likely to be encountered in Britain and adjacent parts of north-western Europe, and provides an introduction to the thousands of species growing in the area. For ease of reference, flowers of similar structure, ranging from the simple to the complex, have been grouped together so that comparisons and distinctions can be made. The whole plant is shown from the ground upwards, except where just a flowering or fruiting shoot is more informative. In addition, close-up details of individual flowers and fruits are given to make identification more accurate.

It is important to take the book to the plant so that, with the use of the keys and comparison with the descriptions and illustrations, it can be identified in its natural surroundings. Never destroy a plant by bringing it home for identification; wild flowers are becoming ever scarcer and it is vital to conserve their fragile beauty for future generations.

How to Identify Wild Flowers

A plant is identified by careful observation of the way it grows and looks, with attention being paid to details of its stems, leaves, flowers and fruit. Plants may grow and flower in a single year (annual), or flower only in the second year (biennial), or over many years (perennial). Stems are variously upright, creeping or climbing, with the leaves either all growing at the base of the plant or along the stems. Stem-leaves may be arranged spirally, in pairs, or in rings. Their general outline, the shape of the tip or base, and details of the edge are all important distinguishing features; many leaves are lobed or divided into leaflets.

Flowers are usually the most obvious feature of these plants and provide the most important characteristics for identification. The main parts of the flower include petals, sepals, stamens and ovaries; the relative size of these parts, their number and the degree to which they are joined should all be taken into account. Petals are generally the largest, most attractive part of flowers; beneath these are usually several green sepals. Sometimes both petals and sepals are similar and then together are termed the *perianth*. Within the petals and sepals are the pollen-producing *stamens*, the male parts of the flowers. The female parts of the flower are the *ovaries*, each with one or more pollen-receptive *stigmas* often borne on a stalk-like part called the *style*. Flowers usually have both male and female parts and are termed *hermaphrodite*, but there may be separate male and female flowers, sometimes on different plants. Seeds develop in the fertilised ovary, which ripens and turns into the fruit. This can be juicy and berry-like, or dry. The latter types of fruit may open by pores or by splitting, or remain closed and nut-like.

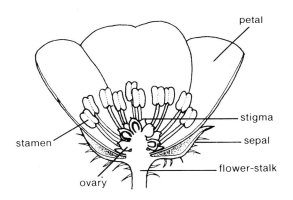

Large coloured petals serve an important biological function, as they are attractive to insects which transfer the pollen from stamens to stigmas, thus achieving fertilisation. But flowers can also be pollinated by the wind, and these types are usually green or brown and small. Flowers may grow singly but they are often clustered together into heads; plants of the Carrot family, for example, usually have distinctive umbrella-shaped flower-heads. In relatives of the Daisy, the 'flower' is actually a very compact head of numerous tiny flowers.

Families of Wild Flowers

The species in this book are grouped into 52 families according to shared characteristics, some of which are described here.

Hops, Nettles and Mistletoes The separate male and female plants have small flowers and commonly have paired leaves. Hops are climbers; the cone-like fruit has papery scales. Nettles mostly have stinging leaves but some species are stingless. Mistletoe is a parasite on branches of trees.

Goosefoots and Docks Most have small, hermaphrodite flowers and alternating leaves. The small dry fruit is covered by the remains of the flower. Goosefoots, often with succulent stems and leaves, include many plants of salt-marshes. Docks have stipules forming a papery tube.

Pinks These typically have paired leaves and flowers with 5 separate, equal petals. The fruit is a capsule.

Water-lilies and Buttercups These mostly have leaves alternating along the stem. Five or more petals are common and there are numerous stamens. Water-lilies have only one ovary; they are water plants with floating leaves. Most Buttercups have numerous ovaries.

Poppies, Cabbages and Fumitories The 4 separate petals are equal, except in Fumitories. Poppies have many stamens, Cabbages 6 and Fumitories only 2. Cabbages have pod-like fruits with two halves detaching leaving a thin inner wall; Poppies often have capsules; the small fruit of Fumitories usually does not open.

Sundews, Stonecrops and Saxifrages These plants typically have 5 equal, separate petals. Sundews and Saxifrages have a single capsule but Stonecrops have a cluster. The leaves of Stonecrops are succulent but those of Sundews have movable, sticky hairs which catch insects.

Roses Many species are woody; most have alternating leaves with a pair of stipules. The flowers typically have 5 equal, separate petals and many stamens. Fruits can be berry-like or dry and nut-like, and are often borne in a cluster.

Peas The flowers usually have a large upper petal, 2 smaller side petals and a pair of lower petals joined around the 10 stamens, ovary and stigma. The fruit is typically a pod which splits lengthwise.

Wood-sorrels, Flaxes and Crane's-bills All have 5 equal, separate petals, but their fruits differ: Wood-sorrels have a capsule that splits open violently lengthwise; Flaxes have a capsule that splits radially; Crane's-bills have a beak-like capsule with 5 segments splitting away with a tail from the beak.

Milkworts and Spurges These are two rather different families. Milkworts carry 3-petalled flowers flanked by 2 large petal-like sepals and 3 smaller sepals. In Spurges, the tiny male flowers encircle the female flower and are held in a cup-like base. The capsule often splits explosively. Most Spurges have a milky, caustic sap.

Mallows, St John's-worts and Violets These plants have 5 separate petals, which are equal in all but the Violets. Mallows and St John's-worts have many stamens but Violets only 5. Capsules occur except in Mallows, where the fruit splits radially into segments.

Loosestrifes and Willowherbs Willowherbs have the ovary beneath the base of the 2 or 4 petals, whereas in Loosestrifes the ovary is at about the same level as its 6 petals. Both have capsules; in Willowherbs these split to release plumed seeds.

Ivies and Carrots Commonly, many 5-petalled flowers are borne in umbrella-shaped heads. Ivy is a woody climber with berry-like fruits. Carrot family species are usually not woody and the dry fruit splits into 2 halves.

Heathers, Primroses and Thrifts Flowers of these families usually have 4 or 5 joined petals. Capsules with many seeds form the normal fruit, but Thrift has a tiny capsule hidden by the remains of the flower and only a single seed.

Gentians and Bedstraws All have 5 equal petals which are joined, making a tubular flower. Gentians have a capsule with many tiny seeds. Native Bedstraws have rings of leaves and leaf-like stipules; the fruit splits into 2 1-seeded halves.

Bindweeds, Forget-me-nots, Mints and Nightshades All but Mints typically have alternating leaves and tubular or funnel-shaped flowers with 5 equal, joined petals. Forget-me-nots and Mints have fruits with 4 nut-like parts. Bindweeds have a capsule and Nightshades usually a berry. Mints have 4-angled stems, paired leaves and unequal petals.

Figworts, Broomrapes and Bladderworts The flowers usually have 5 joined, unequal petals; sometimes 2 are completely joined. The fruits are capsules. Broomrapes lack green pigment; they are parasites on roots. Bladderworts have leaves which catch insects.

Introduction

Plantains, Honeysuckles and Moschatel Plantains have elongated spikes of small, brownish flowers with long stamens. The flowers are followed by capsules. The other two families have rounded flower-heads and berry-like fruits. Honeysuckles have long, tubular 5-petalled flowers. Low-growing Moschatel has heads of 5 flowers, 4 facing apart and one on top.

Teasels, Valerians and Bellflowers In these families, 5 petals are joined to make a tubular flower, or are bell-shaped in Bellflowers. The 2 to 5 stamens are separate and a single ovary is below the base of the petals and sepals. Flowers of Teasels are tightly clustered into compact heads.

Daisies Tiny flowers (florets) are clustered in compact heads, which look like individual flowers. The individual florets have 5 joined petals and are either formed as a tube (disc floret) or a tube with a long, flat lobe attached (ray floret). The Daisy has a mixture of both types, the ray florets being on the outer edge of the flower-head. Stamens are joined to form a tube.

Water-plantains, Lilies, Irises and Lords-and-Ladies The leaves have several veins running from the base. The parts of the perianth are arranged in multiples of three. Water-plantains have several ovaries; the one ovary of Lilies is above the base of the petals while that of Irises is below. Lords-and-Ladies have tiny flowers in a spike, within a large, petal-like hood.

Orchids These have similar leaves with parallel veins. The curious flowers have 3 unequal petals and 3 sepals with the ovary beneath. The stigma and stamens are joined as a central columnar structure.

The Flower Keys

The key to species provides a lead into the individual keys which follow. Every step of the species key consists of two contrasting statements. These should first be checked against the plant to see which one applies. When a correct statement is reached, refer to the number at the end of the line. This will lead to another pair of statements (number in **bold** type, e.g. **2**) or to one of the secondary keys (e.g. Key 1) and thus in turn to a particular species and page number (e.g. Hop 22). Some plants are more variable than others and may fit both statements in a pair. Such species are keyed out twice, so either 'pathway' through the keys may be taken.

Key to Species

1   Flowers green or brown, usually without distinct petals   Key 1
    Flowers with distinct petals, not green or brown   **2**

2   Flowers in very compact, rounded heads, appearing as a single
    flower   Key 2
    Flowers not in very compact, rounded heads   **3**

3   Flowers in broad, flat-topped or umbrella-shaped clusters
    Carrots 57–59
    Flowers not in broad, flat-topped clusters   **4**

4   Petals of different sizes   Key 3
    Petals all the same size   **5**

5   Flowers with less than 5 petals   Key 4
    Flowers with 5 or more petals   **6**

6   Petals joined above the base   Key 5
    Petals separate to the base   **7**

7   Leaves on stems, in pairs or clusters at same level   Key 6
    Leaves all at base of plant or scattered around stem   Key 7

Key 1

1   Plants climbing   **2**
    Plants not climbing   **5**

2   Leaves paired, on opposite sides of stem   **3**
    Leaves spirally arranged or on alternate sides of stem   **4**

3   Stems twining; leaves deeply lobed, leaf-stalk not twining   Hop 22
    Stems not twining; leaves with leaflets and twining stalks
    Traveller's-joy 33

4   Stems woody, often rooting; flowers in rounded head   Ivy 56
    Stems not woody or rooting; flowers in elongated head
    Black-bindweed 24

5   Broken base of leaf exudes a thick, milky sap   Sun Spurge 51
    Sap not milky   **6**

Introduction

Key 2

1 Edges of leaves with strong spines **2**
Edges of leaves without strong spines **3**

2 Stems smooth; leaves rounded, bluish Sea-holly **56**
Stems with winged angles; leaves elongated, dark green
Spear Thistle **88**

3 Leaves mostly paired on stems **4**
Leaves on alternating sides of stem or all at base **6**

4 Flower-head yellow Trifid Bur-marigold **82**
Flower-head bluish or purplish-pink **5**

5 Stem-leaves lobed, bases of leaf pair separate Field Scabious **79**
Stem-leaves not lobed, bases of leaf pair joined Teasel **79**

6 Flower-head with tubular, papery collar beneath Thrift **62**
Flower-head without collar beneath **7**

7 Leaves with 3 rounded leaflets Peas **45–46**
Leaves without leaflets or more than 3 leaflets **8**

8 Sap milky; florets all with long, flattened tip **9**
Sap not milky; at least inner florets tubular **13**

9 Leaves very slender, not lobed Goat's-beard **91**
Leaves not very slender, deeply lobed **10**

10 Stems distinctly leafy; leaves not in tuft at base **11**
Stems more or less leafless; leaves in tuft at base **12**

11 Stems smooth; fruit lacks stalk beneath parachute of hairs
Smooth Sow-thistle **89**
Stems bristly, fruit with stalk beneath parachute of hairs
Beaked Hawk's-beard **90**

12 Stems solid, branched, scaly above; several flower-heads
Cat's-ear **90**
Stems hollow, not branched or scaly; 1 flower-head
Common Dandelion **91**

13 Fruits (and floret base) with parachute of hairs or bristles **14**
Fruits (and floret base) without a parachute **22**

14 Flowering stems scaly, leaves from underground stems later **15**
Flowering stems leafy, no leaves from underground stems **16**

Introduction

Key 3

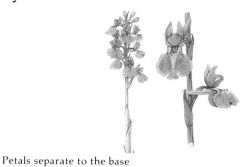

1	Petals separate to the base		**2**
	Petals joined above base forming a tube		**17**
2	Ovary (becomes fruit) beneath base of petals and sepals		**3**
	Ovary (becomes fruit) within petals and sepals		**7**
3	Leaves sword-shaped; flowers point upwards	Yellow Iris	**94**
	Leaves not sword-shaped; flowers horizontal		**4**
4	Leaves spotted; flowers purple		**5**
	Leaves not spotted; flowers white or yellow		**6**
5	Stems distinctly leafy	Common Spotted-orchid	**96**
	Stems only with scale-like leaves	Early-purple Orchid	**96**

6 Spirally arranged leaves; lower petal with long spur
Greater Butterfly-orchid 95
Large pair of leaves; lower petal without spur
Common Twayblade 95

7 Plant with pea-flowers: lowest 2 petals joined,
    boat-shaped, overlapped by 2 side petals, upper petal largest   **8**
Plant does not have pea-flowers   **15**

8	Leaves ending in a tendril		**9**
	Leaves not ending in a tendril		**11**

9 Leaves with 1 pair of leaflets, stipules of similar size
Meadow Vetchling 45
Leaves with many pairs of leaflets, stipules much smaller   **10**

10	Many flowers in slender spike	Tufted Vetch	**44**
	Flowers single or paired at leaf base	Common Vetch	**44**
11	Flowers yellow		**12**
	Flowers white or purplish		**14**
12	Leaflets toothed	Black Medick	**45**
	Leaflets not toothed		**13**

13 Hairy; most leaves with many leaflets, stipules small
Kidney Vetch 47
Almost hairless; leaves with 3 leaflets, stipules same size
Common Bird's-foot-trefoil 47

Introduction

Key 4

1	Flowers with less than 4 petals	**2**
	Flowers with 4 petals	**4**
2	Flowers with single petal-like hood Lords-and-Ladies	**94**
	Flowers with more than 1 petal	**3**
3	Woodland plant; flowers with 2 petals Enchanter's-nightshade	**54**
	Plant of water margin; flowers with 3 petals Water-plantain	**92**
4	Aquatic plant with submerged and floating leaves	**5**
	Land plant, leaves not submerged or floating	**6**
5	Submerged leaves finely divided, floating leaves lobed	
	Common Water-crowfoot	**31**
	Submerged leaves not divided, floating leaves not lobed	
	Water-lilies	**30**
6	Leaves in rings around stem Bedstraws	**63**
	Leaves paired or scattered around stem	**7**
7	Petals joined above base Water Mint	**71**
	Petals separate to base	**8**
8	Flowers with 10 or more stamens	**9**
	Flowers with less than 10 stamens	**12**
9	Flowers yellow	**10**
	Flowers white or red	**11**
10	Sap orange; leaves with paired leaflets Greater Celandine	**34**
	Sap clear; leaves with radiating leaflets and lobes Tormentil	**43**
11	Climbing plant, flowers white Traveller's-joy	**33**
	Plant not climbing, flowers red Common Poppy	**34**
12	Ovary (becomes fruit) beneath base of petals and sepals	
	Willowherbs	**55**
	Ovary (becomes fruit) within petals and sepals	**13**
13	Leaves closely overlapping, edge unbroken Heather	**60**
	Leaves separate, toothed, lobed or with leaflets	**14**
14	Fruits much longer than wide	**15**
	Fruits about as long as wide	**18**
15	Plant bristly; fruit with seedless part at tip	**16**
	Plant with few, soft hairs; fruit with seeds to tip	**17**
16	Lower leaves lobed; sepals spread apart Charlock	**37**
	Lower leaves with separate leaflets; sepals upright Wild Radish	**37**
17	Leaves kidney-shaped or triangular Garlic Mustard	**35**
	Leaves with separate leaflets Cuckooflower	**35**
18	Fruit heart-shaped Shepherd's-purse	**36**
	Fruit circular Field Penny-cress	**36**

Key 5

1 Leaves on stems, in pairs or clusters at same level **2**
Leaves all at base of plant or scattered around stem **4**

2 Leaves divided into toothed leaflets   Common Valerian **80**
Leaves with edge unbroken **3**

3 Flowers single from leaf-base, red, rarely blue or purple
    Scarlet Pimpernel **60**
Flowers in branched heads, pink or rarely white
    Common Centaury **62**

4 Plants climbing or trailing **5**
Plants not climbing or trailing **7**

5 Petals joined at base, curved backwards, purple   Bittersweet **71**
Petals joined to tips, funnel-shaped, pink or white **6**

6 Flowers white   Hedge Bindweed **64**
Flowers pink, white-banded   Field Bindweed **64**

7 Fruit splits into 4 small, nut-like parts (ovary 4-lobed) **8**
Fruit does not split into 4 parts (ovary not 4-lobed) **10**

8 Flowers purple, pink or yellowish-white   Common Comfrey **66**
Flowers blue **9**

9 Petal-tube long, curved   Bugloss **65**
Petal-tube very short, straight   Field Forget-me-not **65**

10 Flower blue; ovary beneath base of petals and sepals   Harebell **80**
Flower yellow or pink; ovary above base of petals and sepals **11**

11 Flowers in a long, slender head   Great Mullein **72**
Flowers solitary or in rounded head **12**

12 Leaves grass-like, not toothed; flowers pinkish   Thrift **62**
Leaves oval or oblong, toothed; flowers usually yellow **13**

13 Flowers single from base of plant   Primrose **61**
Flowers in stalked, 1-sided head   Cowslip **61**

Key 6

1	Leaves with edge toothed, lobed or with separate leaflets	**2**
	Leaves with edge unbroken	**4**
2	Leaves with paired leaflets　　　　　　Common Stork's-bill	50
	Leaves with radiating lobes but not distinct leaflets	**3**
3	Flowers bluish, large　　　　　　　　Meadow Crane's-bill	49
	Flowers purplish-pink, small　　　　　　　　Herb-Robert	49
4	Flowers in slender spikes; 6 petals　　　Purple-loosestrife	54
	Flowers in widely branched heads or solitary; 5 petals	**5**
5	Flowers yellow; more than 10 stamens　Perforate St John's-wort	52
	Flowers white, pink or purplish-pink; 10 or fewer stamens	**6**
6	Sepals joined forming a tube	**7**
	Sepals separate to base	**9**
7	Petals with 4 very narrow lobes　　　　　Ragged-Robin	28
	Petals with 2 broad lobes	**8**
8	Flowers white　　　　　　　　　　　White Campion	29
	Flowers deep pink　　　　　　　　　　Red Campion	29
9	Petals 2-lobed at tip	**10**
	Petals not lobed at tip	**12**
10	Leaves hairy; 5 stigmas and styles　　Common Mouse-ear	27
	Leaves more or less hairless; 3 stigmas and styles	**11**
11	Leaves narrow, stalkless; sepals longer than petals　Greater Stitchwort	26
	Leaves broad, lower stalked; sepals shorter than petals　Common Chickweed	26
12	Leaves very slender, succulent; flowers pink　Greater Sea-spurrey	28
	Leaves not very slender or succulent; flowers white	**13**
13	Leaves pointed; sepals longer than petals　Thyme-leaved Sandwort	27
	Leaves more or less blunt; sepals shorter than petals　Fairy Flax	48

Key 7

21

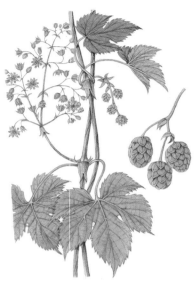

Hop *Humulus lupulus* A tough, bristly, perennial vine used to give bitter taste to beer. Stems twine clockwise up to 600cm. Leaves 100-150mm, paired on stem, stalked, with 3-5 sharply pointed, toothed lobes. Flowers July–August. Male and female flowers on different plants. Male flowers 5mm, in branched clusters, green, with 5-parted perianth and 5 stamens; female flowers form oval, yellowish-green heads 15-20mm long, each has an undivided perianth and 2 stigmas. Fruiting heads 30-50mm, cone-like with papery scales enclosing nut-like fruits. Grows in hedges or bushes, or cultivated on strings held up by tall poles.

Common Nettle *Urtica dioica* The stinging hairs that cover most of the plant make touching this species a painful experience. A perennial with stiffly upright stems 30-150cm tall. Leaves 40-80mm, paired on stem, oval, pointed, sharply toothed and stalked. Flowers June–August. Male and female flowers on different plants. Numerous tiny green flowers form branched clusters. Each flower 1.5-2mm, with 4 perianth-lobes. Male flowers have 4 stamens; female flowers 1 feathery stigma. Fruits 1-1.5mm, oval, nut-like yellowish, each enclosed by a withered flower. Grows in hedgerows, woods and disturbed ground.

Mistletoe *Viscum album*
Leathery, yellowish foliage of
this unusual parasitic plant
grows directly from a tree. A
perennial with woody,
forking, green stems 20-100cm
tall. Leaves 50-80mm, paired
on stem, narrow, tapered
below, sometimes curved,
blunt, with an unbroken edge.
Flowers February–April. Male
and female flowers on
different plants; 3-5 greenish-
yellow flowers, 2-6mm long,
form small cluster at tip of
stem. Male flowers have 4
stamens; female flowers 4
triangular petals and 1 stigma.
Berries are 6-10mm, white,
almost globular, with sticky
flesh surrounding the seed.
Grows mainly on deciduous
trees. Absent from parts of
north and east.

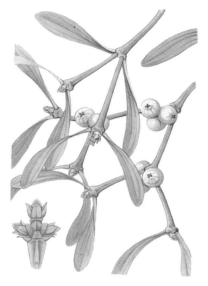

Fat-hen *Chenopodium album*
Common annual weed that
used to be cultivated for edible
leaves and seeds. Stems
10-150cm, upright, slightly
ridged, often striped pink or
white and with small, swollen
hairs that make plant look as
if dusted with flour. Leaves
12-82mm, spirally arranged on
stem, stalked, diamond or
spear-shaped, sometimes
toothed. Flowers July–
October. Many pale green,
hermaphrodite flowers form
spike-like heads; each flower
1.5mm, with 5-parted perianth
of oval lobes, 5 stamens and 2
stigmas. Fruit 1.3-2mm, forms
papery layer over seed, which
is black with faint, radiating
grooves. Grows on cultivated
or waste ground.

Docks

Redshank *Polygonum persicaria*
An annual weed with distinctive dark mark on the leaves. Branched stems 20-80cm tall, upright and swollen above each leaf. Leaves, 50-150mm, on alternate sides of stem, spear-shaped, with an unbroken edge. Flowers June–October. Numerous, hermaphrodite, flowers each 3-5mm form cylindrical, crowded spikes, with 5 petal-like, bright or pale pink parts to the perianth, 8 stamens and 2-3 stigmas. Fruit 2-3mm, nut-like, angular, usually with 2 rounded faces, shiny, enclosed by the withered flower. Grows mainly on waste or cultivated ground; also by water.

Black-bindweed *Fallopia convolvulus* This climbing annual is often a weed of grain crops and used to be eaten itself. Stems 30-120cm, angular. Leaves 20-60mm, on alternate sides of stem, triangular or arrow-shaped, stalked, pointed, with an unbroken edge and rather floury look beneath. Flowers July–October. Hermaphrodite flowers, 4-6mm greenish-white, with short, jointed stalk; the perianth usually with 5 petal-like parts, becoming enlarged and ridged or winged, 8 stamens and 2-3 stigmas. Fruit 4-5mm, nut-like, 3-angled, enclosed by the withered flower, with single, rough, black seed. Grows mainly on waste or cultivated ground.

Sheep's Sorrel *Rumex acetosella*
A small-flowered plant with distinctively lobed leaves often tinged deep crimson. A perennial with upright stems 30cm tall. Leaves up to 40mm, on alternate sides of stem, stalked, pointed, with 2 lobes that curve forwards at the base. Flowers May–August. Male and female flowers on different plants. Numerous flowers form long, branched clusters. Male flowers 2mm, green, becoming crimson, with a 6-parted perianth and 6 stamens; female flowers 1.5-2mm, with 3 feathery stigmas. Fruit 1.3-1.5mm, nut-like, 3-angled, enclosed by a withered flower. Grows on heaths, grassland or cultivated ground.

Broad-leaved Dock *Rumex obtusifolius* Well-known for soothing nettle stings, this robust, upright perennial is 60-120cm tall. Leaves up to 250mm, scattered on stem, blunt with fine-toothed wavy edge. Lower leaves long-stalked and oblong; upper leaves short-stalked and tapered. Flowers June–October. Numerous small, hermaphrodite flowers form rings around upper stem. Each flower 3mm, green and white or crimson, with a 6-parted perianth that develops corky swellings, 6 stamens and 3 stigmas. Fruit 5-6mm, nut-like, enclosed by a withered flower. Grows in woods, hedges and on cultivated and waste ground. Not common in extreme north and south.

Pinks

Common Chickweed *Stellaria media* An annual weed, with weak stems that often flop over. Stems 5-40cm tall, branched with 2 lines of hairs. Leaves 3-25mm, paired on stem, oval, pointed, with an unbroken edge; only lower leaves have stalks. Flowers January–December. Flowers insignificant, white, hermaphrodite; form loose clusters near tip of stem. Each flower has 5 sepals 4.5-5mm, oval and stickily hairy; 5 petals shorter than sepals, with 2 lobes, 5 stamens and 3 stigmas. Capsule egg-shaped or oblong, 5-6mm long, splits into six, releasing many small, rough seeds. Grows mainly on cultivated or waste ground.

Greater Stitchwort *Stellaria holostea* A perennial with 4-angled stems 15-60cm tall, turning upwards from a very slender, weak base. Leaves 40-80mm, paired on stem, spear-shaped, stalkless, slightly bluish with distinctive rough edge. Flowers April–June. Flowers 20-30mm, white, long-stalked, forming loose, leafy heads. Each flower has 5 spear-shaped, pointed sepals 6-9mm; 5 petals 8-12mm, cut into 2 lobes, with 10 stamens and 3 stigmas. Fruit 6-8mm, a globular capsule splitting into six, releasing many small, rough seeds. Grows in woods or hedges.

Thyme-leaved Sandwort
Arenaria serpyllifolia
A sprawling annual or biennial, with stems that turn upwards. Stems 2.5-25cm, slender and hairy. Leaves 2.5-8mm, paired on stem, oval, pointed, grey-green, with an unbroken edge; only lower leaves are stalked. Flowers June–August. Numerous small, white, hermaphrodite flowers form widely branched heads. Each flower 5-8mm, stalked; 5 sepals, 3-4.5mm, spear-shaped; 5 equal, oval, undivided petals are shorter than sepals; with 10 stamens and 3 stigmas. Fruit 4mm, an oval capsule, opening to release numerous small, blackish, rough seeds. Grows in arable fields, on downs, cliffs or walls. Not common in extreme north.

Common Mouse-ear *Cerastium fontanum* A trailing perennial forming extensive loose tufts. Stems 5-50cm long, turn upright to flower, densely covered with soft, white hairs. Leaves 10-25mm, paired on stem, no stalk, spear-shaped; lower leaves blunt, upper leaves pointed. Flowers April–September. Flowers hermaphrodite, white, stalked, in branched heads. Each flower 7-10mm, 5-7 sepals 3-5mm, oval, broad-based, hairy except for tip; 5 petals with 2 lobes, 10 stamens and 5 stigmas. Fruit 9-12mm, a cylindrical, curved capsule, opens to release numerous small, kidney-shaped, reddish-brown, rough seeds. Grows in grassy places, shingle and dunes.

Pinks

Greater Sea-spurrey
Spergularia media A succulent perennial of the drier parts of salt-marshes. Stems 10-35cm, low growing, angled upwards. Leaves 10-25mm, paired on stem, not stalked, narrow, straight-sided, fleshy, blunt or sharp. Flowers June–September. Flowers 7.5-12mm, hermaphrodite, stalked, pink or whitish, in loose, widely branched heads; 5 sepals 4-5mm, sometimes stickily hairy; 5 petals 4.5-5.5mm, oval, undivided, with 10 stamens and 3 stigmas. Fruit 7-11mm, a capsule splitting into three to release many round, yellowish-brown seeds. Each seed 1.5mm, encircled by a pale wing. Grows in mud or sand of salt-marshes.

Ragged-Robin *Lychnis flos-cuculi*
An upright perennial 20-90cm tall; the branched stems have sparse, stiff hairs. Leaves 20-100mm, paired on stem, slightly rough; lower leaves oblong, pointed, stalked, upper spear-shaped, base of each pair joined together. Flowers May–June. Flowers hermaphrodite, red, stalked, in widely branched heads. Each flower 30-40mm wide; 5 reddish sepals 6-10mm, joined into a 10-veined tube; 5 petals with 4 narrow lobes, 10 stamens and 5 stigmas. Fruit 6-10mm, a capsule, opening to release many kidney-shaped, rough, brown seeds. Grows on damp soils of meadows, fens, marshes, or wet woods. Not common in south.

White Campion *Silene alba*
A softly hairy perennial, with
upright, branched stems
30-100cm tall. Leaves
30-100mm, paired on stem,
spear-shaped; only lower
leaves have stalks. Flowers
May–September. Flowers
25-30mm, creamy white,
stalked, form stickily hairy,
branched heads; open in
evening to attract moths. Male
and female flowers on different
plants. Flowers have 5 sepals
in a tube 18-25mm long;
5 petals with 2 lobes; male
flowers 10 stamens, female
flowers 5 stigmas. Fruit 15mm,
an egg-shaped capsule, opens
to release many small, kidney-
shaped, grey, rough seeds.
Grows on cultivated or waste
ground and by hedges.

Red Campion *Silene dioica*
A softly hairy perennial, with
upright stems 20-90cm tall.
Leaves 40-100mm, paired on
stem, oval, pointed; lower
leaves have a winged stalk.
Flowers May–June. Male and
female flowers on different
plants. Each flower 18-25mm,
rose-pink, scentless, with stalk
5-15mm; 5 sepals 12-17.5mm,
joined into tube with sharp,
triangular teeth; 5 petals with
2 lobes. Male flowers have 10
stamens; female flowers 5
stigmas. Fruit 10-15mm, an
egg-shaped capsule opening to
release many small, black,
kidney-shaped, rough seeds.
Grows in woods, hedges,
screes and cliffs. Not common
in extreme south.

Water-lilies

Yellow Water-lily *Nuphar lutea*
An aquatic perennial with horizontal, submerged stems, 30-80mm in diameter. Leaves 120-400mm, mostly floating, broadly oval with deep cleft, leathery, green above and below, with stalk up to 300cm; submerged leaves thin and translucent. Flowers June–August. Flowers 40-60mm, hermaphrodite, yellow, globular, on long stalks above surface of water; 4-6 sepals 20-30mm, oval; numerous petals smaller than sepals, with many stamens and 15-20 stigmas. Fruit 35-60mm, smells of alcohol, globular with a narrowed neck, splits to release many seeds, each 5mm. Grows in lakes, ponds, canals, and slow rivers.

White Water-lily *Nymphaea alba* An aquatic perennial with short, stout, horizontal, submerged stems. Leaves 100-300mm, from base of plant, circular with deep cleft, floating, dark glossy green above, usually reddish below, with stalk up to 300cm. Flowers July–August. Flowers 50-200mm, hermaphrodite, cup-shaped, floating, scented, white with stalk up to 300cm; 4 sepals spear-shaped, white inside; 20-25 petals spirally arranged, with many stamens and stigmas. Fruit 16-40mm spongy, oval to nearly globular, splitting underwater to release many floating seeds, each 3mm. Grows in lakes and ponds.

Marsh-marigold *Caltha palustris*
A perennial with upright
hollow stems up to 30cm tall.
Leaves 50-150mm, at base of
plant or scattered around
stem, kidney-shaped or
triangular, blunt, toothed, the
base heart-shaped; lower
leaves have long stalks.
Flowers March–July. Flowers
16-50mm, hermaphrodite,
golden, cup-shaped, long-
stalked, in a widely branched
head. Each flower has
perianth with 5-8 equal parts,
50-100 stamens and 5-15
stigmas. Fruits 9-18mm, pod-
like, upright or spreading
apart, splitting along inner
face to release many small
seeds, each up to 2.5mm.
Grows in ditches, damp
woods, and marshes.

Common Water-crowfoot
Ranunculus aquatilis An
amphibious perennial,
submerged, floating or low-
growing on land, with long,
branched stems. Leaves
30-60mm, spirally arranged on
stem. Submerged leaves with
fine, hair-like segments;
floating leaves or those on
land with 3-7 toothed lobes.
Flowers May–June. Flowers
12-18mm, hermaphrodite,
buttercup-like, with stalk
20-50mm; 5 sepals; 5 equal
petals 5-10mm, white with
yellow base; 13 or more
stamens, many stigmas.
Numerous fruits form a
rounded head; each fruit
1.5-2mm, nut-like, egg-shaped
with curved tip, ridged, hairy,
does not open. Grows in
ponds, streams or ditches.

Buttercups

Meadow Buttercup *Ranunculus acris* Plentiful in pastures, this perennial has upright, branched, hollow stems up to 100cm tall. Leaves 50-120mm, from base or alternate sides of stem; lower leaves long-stalked, with 2-7 toothed lobes; upper leaves with narrow lobes, and often stalkless. Flowers June–July. Flowers hermaphrodite, glossy yellow, cup-shaped. Each flower 18-25mm, stalked; 5 sepals oval, hairy; 5 or more equal petals each 6-11mm, with many stamens and stigmas. Fruit 2.5-3mm, nut-like, smooth, egg-shaped with a hooked tip, does not open to release seed; many fruits together in rounded head. Grows in damp meadows and other grassy places.

Lesser Celandine *Ranunculus ficaria* Carpeting the spring woodland floor with gold, this perennial is 5-25cm tall, with stems angled upwards. Leaves 10-40mm, from base or spirally arranged on stem, heart-shaped, toothed, with notch in base of leaf; lower leaves have longer stalks than upper leaves. Flowers March–May. Rich yellow flowers 20-30mm, hermaphrodite, singly on long stalks; 3 sepals oval; 8-12 petals oval; many stamens and stigmas. Fruit up to 2.5mm, broadly egg-shaped, beaked, does not open to release seed. Many fruits together in rounded heads. Grows in woods, hedges or grassy banks.

Wood Anemone *Anemone nemorosa* Often in great profusion on woodland floor, this perennial has upright, unbranched stems up to 30cm tall. Leaves 20-40mm, on alternate sides of stem with one or two from base after flowering. Lower leaves, long-stalked with 3 spreading, toothed lobes; stem-leaves short-stalked. Flowers March–May. Flowers 20-40mm, hermaphrodite, stalked, singly at tip of stem, cup-shaped, white often tinged purple; perianth has 5-9 equal lobes; many stamens and stigmas. Fruit 4-4.5mm, nut-like, egg-shaped, beaked, downy, does not open to release seed; up to 30 fruits form nodding, rounded heads. Grows in deciduous woods.

Traveller's-joy *Clematis vitalba* A robust, perennial vine with thick, woody, rope-like stems up to 30m tall. Leaves paired on stem; each leaf with one or two pairs of oval, pointed, toothed leaflets 30-100mm long and a leaflet or tendril at tip; the leaf-stalk twines. Flowers July–August. Flowers hermaphrodite, fragrant, greenish-white, in a branched head. Each flower 20mm, stalked; the perianth usually has 4 lobes; many stamens and several stigmas. Fruit 15-25mm, feathery, white-plumed, with nut-like base not opening to release the seed; forms fluffy masses. Grows in woods or hedges.

Poppies

Common Poppy *Papaver rhoeas*
Familiar for turning cornfields
and roadsides blood-red, this
bristly annual grows 20-60cm
tall, with upright, branched
stems exuding milky sap when
cut. Leaves 20-150mm, lower
stalked, with narrow, toothed
segments; upper stem-leaves
mostly stalkless and 3-lobed.
Flowers June–August. Flowers
70-100mm, hermaphrodite,
often with black blotches; as
crumpled petals open, both
sepals fall; 4 circular petals
20-40mm which soon fall;
many bluish stamens and 8-12
stigmas. Fruit 10-20mm, a
capsule opening by ring of
pores to release many blackish
seeds, each 1mm. Grows in
arable fields, roadsides and
waste places.

Greater Celandine *Chelidonium
majus* Formerly cultivated but
now a weed, this perennial
grows 30-90cm tall. Stem
exudes orange sap when cut.
Leaves 20-250mm, arise from
base or are scattered around
stem; each leaf with 2-3 pairs
of toothed leaflets and leaflet
at tip; only lower leaves are
stalked. Flowers May–August.
Flowers 20-25mm,
hermaphrodite, bright yellow,
stalked; 2 hairy sepals soon
fall; 4 oval petals 10mm; many
yellow stamens and a 2-lobed
stigma. Fruit 30-55mm,
slender, pod-like, splits to
release many tiny black seeds,
each 1.5-2mm, with fleshy,
oily, white outgrowth that
attracts ants. Grows in
hedges, walls and disturbed
ground.

Garlic Mustard *Alliaria petiolata*
Recognised by a garlic-like
aroma, this upright biennial or
perennial grows 20-120cm tall.
Pale green leaves 30-120mm,
from base or spirally arranged
on stem; lower leaves kidney-
shaped, wavy-edged and long-
stalked; stem leaves
triangular, toothed and short-
stalked. Flowers April–June.
About 30 hermaphrodite
flowers, 5-10mm wide, form an
elongated head; 4 sepals
2.5-3.5mm, oval, whitish-
green; 4 petals 4-8mm, snow-
white, rounded, with 6
stamens and 1 stigma. Fruits
35-60mm, pod-like, open to
release 3-18 black seeds, each
3mm long. Grows in woods,
hedges and beneath walls. Not
common in north.

Cuckooflower *Cardamine
pratensis* A perennial 15-60cm
tall, usually with upright
stems. Leaves 15-150mm, from
base or spirally arranged on
stem; lower leaves have
rounded, toothed leaflets;
upper leaves have narrow
leaflets with edge often
unbroken. Flowers April–June.
Flowers hermaphrodite, lilac
or white, in short heads of
7-20 flowers. Each flower
12-18mm; 4 sepals 3-4mm,
often with a violet tip; 4 equal,
oval petals 8-13mm, with
notched tip; 4-6 yellow
stamens and a 2-lobed stigma.
Slender, pod-like fruit is 25-
40mm, suddenly coiling open
to fling out many oblong
seeds, each 2mm. Grows in
damp meadows or by water.

Cabbages

Shepherd's-purse *Capsella bursa-pastoris* A widespread, weedy annual or biennial, 3-40cm tall, with upright, sparsely hairy stems. Leaves 50-200mm, from base or spirally arranged on stem; lower leaves spear-shaped; upper leaves stalkless, with 2 pointed, basal lobes. Flowers at almost any time of year. Small hermaphrodite flowers form elongated heads, each flower 2-3.5mm wide; 4 upright sepals 1-1.5mm; 4 oval, notched petals 2-3mm, with 6 stamens and 1 stigma. Fruits 6-9mm, heart-shaped or triangular, flattened, splitting to release 6-12 oblong, pale brown seeds, each 0.8-1mm long. Grows on cultivated or waste land and roadsides.

Field Penny-cress *Thlaspi arvense* Sometimes a serious pest on farmland, this weedy annual has upright, sparsely branched stems 10-60cm tall. Leaves 20-100mm, oval or spear-shaped, spirally arranged on stem, with unbroken or toothed edge; upper, stalkless leaves clasp stem with pointed lobes. Flowers May–July. Flowers hermaphrodite, form elongated heads, each flower 4-6mm wide; 4 narrow sepals 1.5-2mm; 4 petals, 3-4mm, white, broad, notched; with 6 stamens and a 2-lobed stigma. Fruits 12-22mm, circular, notched, with thin, wing-like edges, splitting to release 5-8 brownish-black seeds, each 1.5-2mm. Grows in arable fields or waste places.

Charlock *Sinapis arvensis* This coarse, bristly annual, 30-80cm tall, is a member of the cabbage family. Leaves spirally arranged on stem; lower leaves up to 200mm long, stalked, with small basal lobes; upper leaves spear-shaped and stalkless. Flowers May–July. Flowers hermaphrodite, cross-shaped, form elongated heads, each flower 12-17mm; 4 sepals spread apart; 4 petals 9-12mm bright yellow, broad, with 6 stamens and a 2-lobed stigma. Fruit 25-40mm, narrow, pod-like, with long, beak-like tip; splits to release 4-12 globular, brown seeds, each 3mm. Grows on arable and waste land.

Wild Radish *Raphanus raphanistrum* Bristly annual, 20-60cm tall, with upright, branched stems. Leaves spirally arranged on stem, with 1-4 pairs of wide-spaced, toothed lobes and a large, blunt top lobe; upper leaves smaller and toothed. Flowers May–September. Flowers 15-22mm, hermaphrodite, stalked, forming narrow heads; 4 upright sepals 5-10mm; 4 petals 12-20mm, yellow or white, tinged with lilac, broad, notched; with 6 stamens and 1 stigma. Fruits 30-90mm, pod-like, with thin beak-like tip, breaking into 3-8 segments each containing a globular, reddish-brown seed, 1.5-3mm long. Grows in arable fields and waste ground.

Fumitories/Sundews

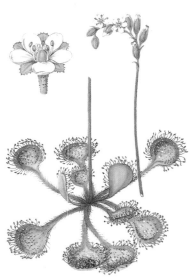

Common Fumitory *Fumaria officinalis* A grey-green, acrid-smelling, hairless annual, 12-40cm tall, with nearly upright or clambering stems. Stalked leaves 20-100mm, spirally arranged on stem and cut into narrow lobes. Flowers May–October. Flowers hermaphrodite, elongated 7-9mm, in spikes of 10-40; 2 oval, pointed sepals 2-3.5mm, toothed at base and soon fall; 4 unequal petals, pink and blackish-purple, held close together, both inner petals hidden by larger, outer petals; with 2 stamens and a 2-lobed stigma. Fruit 2-2.5mm, nut-like, nearly globular; does not open to release the seed. Grows on cultivated and waste ground.

Round-leaved Sundew *Drosera rotundifolia* A slender insectivorous perennial, 6-25cm tall, with a distinctive rosette of leaves covered with glistening red droplets. Leaves 10mm wide, long-stalked, circular and fringed with sticky hairs that curve round to trap insects. Leaves secrete digestive fluid. Flowers June–August. Flowers hermaphrodite, 6-10 forming slender heads; each flower 5mm wide; 5 sepals are toothed; 5 oval, white petals are all equal; with 5 stamens and 3 deeply-forked stigmas. Fruit a capsule; opens to release numerous, small, elongated seeds. Grows in bogs or by water on heaths and moors.

Biting Stonecrop *Sedum acre*
A low-growing perennial of dry,
sunny places, 2-10cm tall, with
branched, rooting stems often
forming mats. Leaves 3-5mm,
stubby, succulent, stalkless,
overlapping, spirally arranged
on stem. Flowers June–July.
Flowers hermaphrodite, 12mm
wide, form few-flowered,
widely branched heads; 5 oval
sepals; 5 spear-shaped, bright
yellow petals 8-9mm; with 10
stamens and 5 stigmas. Fruit
in 5 pointed, pod-like parts
5-6mm long, splits to release
many egg-shaped seeds, each
1mm. Grows on dunes,
shingle, dry, grassy places,
railway tracks and walls. Not
common in parts of north.

Meadow Saxifrage *Saxifraga
granulata* A sparsely hairy
perennial of meadows,
10-50cm tall, with few upright
stems. Leaves 5-30mm, most
from base of plant, long-
stalked kidney-shaped, rather
thick, blunt with rounded
lobes or teeth and heart-
shaped base; the few short-
stalked stem-leaves have
wedge-shaped base. Flowers
April–June. Flowers
hermaphrodite, up to 12
stalked flowers form loosely
branched, stickily hairy head;
5 oval, blunt sepals; 5 oval,
white petals 10-17mm; with 10
stamens and 2 stigmas. Fruit
almost globular, 6-8mm long;
splits to release numerous,
egg-shaped, rough, black
seeds. Grows in grassland.
Scattered mainly in east.

Roses

Dog-rose *Rosa canina* Covered with curved prickles, the arching stems of this woody perennial grow to 3m tall or form tangled thickets. Divided, stalked leaves, on alternate sides of stem, have 2-3 pairs of oval, pointed, toothed leaflets 15-40mm long, and one leaflet at tip. Flowers June–July. Flowers hermaphrodite, 15-25mm, delicately scented; 5 sepals bent backwards; 5 petals 20-25mm broad, pale pink or white; with numerous stamens and many stigmas. Scarlet, berry-like fruit is 10-20mm, globular or egg-shaped, with outer fleshy layer enclosing many nut-like fruits each containing one seed. Grows in woods, scrub and hedges. Not common in north.

Bramble *Rubus fruticosus* Prickly and woody, stems of this perennial reach up to 3m or arch over and root at the tip. Most leaves on alternate sides of stem, divided into 5 oval, pointed, toothed, leaflets, hairy beneath. Flowers June–September. Flowers hermaphrodite, stalked, 20-25mm wide, form cylindrical heads; 5 sepals, oval, pointed, grey-felted and bend backwards; 5 petals, pink or white, equal almost circular; with many stamens and stigmas. Fruit 15-22mm, made up of berry-like segments, ripens from red to black; each segment with a hard centre enclosing a seed. Grows in scrub, hedges or woods.

Meadowsweet *Filipendula ulmaria* Forming large clumps, this perennial grows 60-120cm tall. Leaves on alternate sides of stem; lower leaves long-stalked, 300-600mm, with 2-5 pairs of oval, pointed, toothed leaflets and a 3-lobed leaflet at the tip; dark green, with dense grey hairs below; upper leaves have few leaflets or are undivided. Flowers June–September. Flowers hermaphrodite, 5-10mm, masses of small flowers form frothy, branched heads; 5 triangular, hairy sepals bent backwards; 5 oval petals, 2-5mm long, creamy-white, with 20-40 stamens and 6-10 stigmas. Small fruits 2mm, twisted spirally, each with 2 seeds. Grows on damp ground or by rivers.

Agrimony *Agrimonia eupatoria* Slender, upright stems of this perennial grow 30-60cm tall. Coarse, short-stalked leaves on alternate sides of stem, with 3-6 pairs of elliptical, toothed leaflets 20-60mm long, grey-woolly beneath. Flowers June–August. Flowers hermaphrodite, 5-8mm, form slender spires; 5 sepals are oval, pointed; 5 golden-yellow petals are oval; with 10-20 stamens and 1-2 stigmas. Fruit 6-7mm, conical, broad-topped, leathery, with hooked spines, enclosing 1-2 nut-like parts, each containing a seed. Grows in grassy places, hedges or roadsides. Absent from parts of north.

Roses

Wood Avens *Geum urbanum*
Favouring shady places and often a weed, this perennial grows 20-60cm tall, with upright, brittle, bristly stems. Leaves from base or alternate sides of stem; lower leaves stalked, with 2-4 pairs of leaflets and one at tip, each 5-80mm, toothed or lobed; upper stalkless leaves with up to 3 leaflets or lobes. Flowers June–August. Flowers hermaphrodite, 10-15mm, forming loose, branched heads; 5 sepals are triangular, pointed; 5 petals 5-9mm, yellow oval or oblong; with many stamens and stigmas. Hooked, dry fruits 3-6mm, with nut-like base, retain seed; form spherical heads. Grows in woods and hedges. Absent from parts of north.

Wild Strawberry *Fragaria vesca*
Like a tiny Garden Strawberry, this perennial grows 5-30cm tall, with upright stems or low, arching stems that root to make new plants. Leaves grow from base or scattered on stem, divided into 3 oval, toothed, hairy, leaflets, each 10-60mm. Flowers April–July. Flowers 12-18mm, hermaphrodite; 5 sepals 3-6mm, oval, pointed, spreading or bent backwards; 5 petals 5-7mm, oval, white, with 20 stamens and many stigmas. Tiny, yellowish, nut-like fruits sunk into a juicy, red, globular base, 10-20mm long. Grows in woods, hedges or short grassland.

Silverweed *Potentilla anserina*
Silky and silvery, this
perennial has creeping,
rooting stems up to 80cm long.
Leaves 50-200mm long,
alternate sides of stem, with
short stalks and 7-25 oval or
oblong, toothed leaflets, each
up to 4cm long. Flowers June–
August. Flowers 15-20cm,
hermaphrodite, on long stalks;
5 oval sepals pointed and
surrounded by several
triangular or spear-shaped
bracts; 5 oval petals 7-10mm;
with many stamens and
stigmas. Rounded heads of
small, nut-like fruits each
retain a single seed. Grows in
grassy and waste places and
roadsides.

Tormentil *Potentilla erecta* With
slender, widely branched
stems, this perennial turns
upright from a spreading base
to grow 30cm tall. Radiating,
toothed leaflets are a
distinctive feature of leaves on
alternate sides of stem; each
leaflet 5-20mm long; lower
leaves long-stalked, upper
leaves stalkless. Flowers June–
September. Flowers
7-15mm, hermaphrodite,
buttercup-like; 4 spear-shaped
sepals are encircled by several
bracts; 4 petals 3-6mm, yellow,
rounded, notched; with 14-20
stamens and several stigmas.
Fruits in rounded heads; 4-8
small, egg-shaped, rough, nut-
like fruits each retain a single
seed. Grows on heaths, bogs
or woodland clearings.

Peas

Tufted Vetch *Vicia cracca*
Scrambling and climbing with
its delicate tendrils, this
perennial grows 60-200cm tall.
Ladder-like leaves on alternate
sides of stem, with 6-15 pairs
of leaflets, each 5-30mm long,
spear-shaped, the tip with a
branched tendril. Flowers
June–August. Flowers
10-12mm, hermaphrodite,
form slender, stalked spikes of
10-40 flowers; 5 sepals, 2-4mm
long joined into a tube at base;
5 petals 10-12mm, purple and
blue, the lower pair joined, the
side pair overlapping and the
upper largest; with 10 joined
stamens and 1 stigma. Fruit
10-20mm, an oblong pod, splits
to throw out 2-6 circular
mottled seeds, each 3mm.
Grows in grassy places and
hedges.

Common Vetch *Vicia sativa*
Sometimes an escape from
field crops, this annual grows
15-120cm tall, with climbing or
trailing stems. Leaves on
alternate sides of stem, with
4-8 pairs of pointed or notched
leaflets, each 6-30mm, and a
branched tendril at tip.
Flowers May–September.
Flowers 10-30mm,
hermaphrodite, short-stalked;
5 sepals 6-12mm long, joined
into a tube at the base; 5
petals 10-30mm, purple, the
lower pair joined, the side pair
overlapping and the upper
largest; with 10 joined
stamens and 1 stigma. Fruit an
oblong pod, 25-80mm, splits to
throw out 4-12, globular,
mottled seeds, each 2-6.5mm.
Grows in hedges, grassy
places and arable fields.

Meadow Vetchling *Lathyrus pratensis* Climbing through low shrubs, this perennial has angular stems 30-120cm tall. Leaves 10-30mm, on alternate sides of stem, with a pair of spear-shaped leaflets and a twining tendril at the tip, Flowers May–August. Flowers 15-18mm, hermaphrodite, 5-12 flowers form long-stalked heads; 5 sepals joined into tube at base; 5 petals, yellow, greenish-veined, the lower pair joined, the side pair overlapping and the upper largest; with 10 stamens and 1 stigma. The oblong, blackish pod, 25-35mm long, splits to release 5-10 globular, smooth seeds, each 3-4mm. Grows in grassy places, scrub or hedges.

Black Medick *Medicago lupulina* Rather downy annual or perennial with stems 5-60cm long. Leaves on alternate sides of stem, with 3 oval or circular, toothed leaflets, each 3-20mm with a rounded or notched tip; the end leaflet has a short stalk. Flowers April–August. Flowers 2-3mm, hermaphrodite, up to 50 tiny flowers form rounded, stalked heads 3-8mm long; 5 sepals joined to form a tube; 5 petals, bright yellow, the lower pair joined, the side pair overlapping and the upper largest; with 10 stamens and 1 stigma. The black, kidney-shaped pod is 1.5-3mm long, veined; retains its seed. Grows in grassy places, on sides of roads and paths. Absent from parts of extreme north.

Peas

White Clover *Trifolium repens*
Creeping and rooting, the low-growing stems of this perennial reach up to 50cm long. Long-stalked leaves on alternate sides of stem, each with 3 oval or heart-shaped leaflets 10-30mm long, often marked with white. Flowers June–September. Flowers 8-10mm, hermaphrodite, in globular heads 15-20(-35)mm long; 5 sepals joined at base, bell-shaped, white with green veins, the upper longest; 5 petals 8-10mm, white or pink, the lower pair joined, the side pair overlapping and the upper largest; with 10 stamens and 1 stigma. The pod is 4-5mm, oblong, hairless, covered by the remains of the petals, opening to release 3-6 seeds. Grows in grassy places.

Red Clover *Trifolium pratense*
Often an escape from cultivation, this perennial has almost upright stems 5-100cm tall. Leaves on alternate sides of stem, with 3 elliptical or oval leaflets, 10-30mm long, usually with a V-shaped mark; lower leaves have the longest stalks. Flowers May–September. Flowers 12-15mm, hermaphrodite, in rounded, stalkless heads 20-40mm long, at tip of stem; 5 sepals, with the lowest longest, form a 10-ribbed, hairy tube; 5 petals pinkish-purple, lower pair joined, side pair overlapping and the upper largest; with 10 stamens and 1 stigma. An egg-shaped, hairless pod, 2-2.5mm long, opens to release 1 seed. Grows in grassy places. Not common in parts of north.

Common Bird's-foot-trefoil
Lotus corniculatus Sometimes
forming leafy cushions, this
perennial has low-growing,
wiry stems 10-40cm long.
Leaves on alternate sides of
stem, short-stalked with 5
spear-shaped to nearly
circular leaflets, 4-18mm long.
Flowers June–September.
Flowers 10-16mm,
hermaphrodite, form long-
stalked heads of 2-8, with all
flowers at same level; 5 equal
sepals joined into a tube with
triangular teeth; 5 petals
9-16mm, yellow, streaked red,
the lower pair joined, side pair
overlapping, upper largest;
with 10 stamens and 1 stigma.
Pod cylindrical, 15-30mm; splits
to release several kidney-
shaped seeds, each 1-1.5mm.
Grows in grassy places.

Kidney Vetch *Anthyllis
vulneraria* This hairy perennial
has stems turning upright to
60cm tall. Leaves up to 140mm
on alternate sides of stem,
short-stalked, with 5-15 oval
or oblong, paired leaflets.
Flowers June–September.
Flowers 12-15mm,
hermaphrodite, form compact,
paired heads on a long stalk; 5
unequal sepals form a balloon-
like, woolly tube; 5 petals
yellow or orange, lower pair
joined, side pair overlapping,
and the upper largest; with 10
stamens and 1 stigma. Pod
3mm, nearly globular and
enclosed by sepal-tube,
retaining its 1-2, slightly
notched seeds. Grows in
sunny, grassy places.

Wood-sorrel *Oxalis acetosella*
Often carpeting woodland floor, this perennial has leafless, upright stems 5-15cm tall. Leaves 10-20mm, from base of plant, long-stalked with three heart-shaped, notched leaflets that fold together at night or in wet weather. Flowers April–May. Flowers 5-30mm, solitary and hermaphrodite, delicate, cup-shaped and long-stalked; 5 oblong, blunt sepals 3-4mm; 5 equal petals 8-16mm white, flushed lilac, oval, notched; with 10 stamens and 5 stigmas. Fruit, 4-7mm long, a 5-ridged capsule, splitting to shoot out many egg-shaped, ridged, elastic-coated seeds, each 2-2.5mm long. Grows in woods, hedges or amongst rocks.

Fairy Flax *Linum catharticum*
Delicate and wiry, this relative of cultivated flax has slender, blackish, upright stems 5-25cm tall. Leaves 5-12mm, paired on stem, spear-shaped or oblong, stalkless, with base wedge-shaped or rounded. Flowers June–September. Flowers 5-7mm, hermaphrodite, on hair-like stalks forming widely branched heads, nodding in bud; 5 equal, spear-shaped, pointed sepals 2-3mm, 5 petals 4-6mm, starry white, oval, round-tipped, equal, separate; with 5 stamens and 5 club-shaped stigmas. Fruit 2-3mm, a capsule, nearly globular, splitting into ten parts to release several flattened seeds, each 1mm long. Grows in grassy places, moors and dunes.

Meadow Crane's-bill *Geranium pratense* A robust, upright perennial growing 30-80cm tall. Leaves 70-150mm, from base or on alternate sides of stem, with 3-7 large, radiating, toothed lobes; lower leaves long-stalked, upper leaves almost stalkless. Flowers June–September. Flowers 30-40mm, hermaphrodite; bold, bright, blue-violet, cup-shaped; 5 sepals oval and bristle-tipped; 5 petals, oval, rounded, equal; with 10 stamens and 5 stigmas. Fruit 25-30mm, a capsule, long-beaked, each basal lobe containing a smooth seed which is flung out as the lobe breaks, coiling back like a clock-spring. Grows in grassy, sunny places.

Herb-Robert *Geranium robertianum* Striking when the foliage is flushed with crimson, this annual or biennial has brittle, branched stems, up to 50cm tall. Leaves 15-65mm, from base or paired on stem, deeply cut into 3-5, irregularly paired, toothed lobes. Flowers May–September. Flowers 16-20mm, hermaphrodite, in small, stalked clusters; 5 oval sepals are bristle-tipped; 5 petals purplish-pink, equal, oval, with a slender base; with 10 stamens and 5 stigmas. Fruit 12-20mm, a capsule, long-beaked, with each of 5 basal lobes containing an oblong, smooth seed, lobes detach or remain attached by fibres. Grows in woods and hedges, amongst rocks or on walls.

Common Stork's-bill *Erodium cicutarium* Often stickily hairy, this variable annual has stems creeping or angled upwards from very short to 100cm long. Leaves 20-200mm, mostly paired, with pairs of lobed leaflets. Flowers June–September. Flowers 8-18mm, hermaphrodite, up to 9 flowers form a long-stalked head; 5 oval sepals are pointed; 5 slightly unequal petals are oval, pinkish-purple; with 5 stamens and 5 stigmas. Fruit 15-40mm, a long-beaked capsule, each lobe retains its oblong seed, detaches with a strip from top of beak to form a corkscrew-like coil and slowly twists to bury the seed. Grows on dunes, cultivated or waste ground.

Common Milkwort *Polygala vulgaris* Usually a small plant with stems at various angles, this perennial grows 10-30cm tall. Leaves 5-35mm, scattered around stem, oval or elliptical, pointed, stalkless. Flowers May–September. Flowers 4-8mm, hermaphrodite, 10-40 flowers form spikes; 5 sepals are unequal, with large, inner pair brightly coloured, oval and petal-like; 3 fringed petals bright blue, pink or white, joined into a tube at the base; with 8 stamens and a 2-lobed stigma. Fruit 4-6mm, a capsule, heart-shaped and flattened, splitting along edge to release 2 oblong, hairy seeds, each 2.5-3mm. Grows in grassland, heaths and on dunes.

Dog's Mercury *Mercurialis perennis* Spreading underground to form extensive carpets on woodland floor, this perennial has upright stems 15-40cm tall. Leaves 30-80mm, paired on stem, dark green, elliptical, pointed, toothed. Flowers February–April. Plants are either male or female with green flowers in long-stalked spikes, each with 3 perianth lobes; many male flowers in each spike are 4-5mm, with 8-15 stamens; the few female flowers each have 2 stigmas. Fruit 6-8mm, a broad, hairy capsule, opening to release 2 globular, rough seeds, each 3-3.5mm. Grows in woods and hedges. Not common in extreme north.

Sun Spurge *Euphorbia helioscopia* A curious upright annual with stems 10-50cm tall, exuding milky, caustic sap when cut. Lower leaves 15-30mm, spirally arranged on stem, oval, toothed, stalkless; leaf-like bracts form a ring below flowers. Flowers May–October. Male and female flowers separate, each female flower encircled by several male flowers in a cup-like base with 4 or 5 oval, yellowish glands around the lip; no sepals or petals; with 1 stamen and 3 forked stigmas. Fruit 3-5mm, a smooth capsule, globular, slightly 3-angled, splitting to eject 3 rough brown seeds, each 2mm. Grows on cultivated and waste ground.

Common Mallow *Malva sylvestris* Low-growing to upright stems of this sparsely hairy perennial reach 90cm long. Leaves 50-100mm, from base or spirally arranged on stem, with 5-7 fan-like, slightly folded lobes, with rounded teeth. Flowers June–September. Flowers 25-40mm, hermaphrodite, in small clusters; 5 triangular sepals have 3 extra sepal-like parts; 5 oval petals pinkish-purple with dark stripes, with squarish, notched tips twisted together in bud; with many stamens in a club-shaped head and several stigmas. Fruit is a ring of wedge-shaped, nut-like segments, each with a circular, flattened seed. Grows in grassy places. Absent from parts of north.

Perforate St John's-wort *Hypericum perforatum* Upright stems of this perennial have two fine, raised lines, and grow 30-90cm tall, becoming woody at the base. Leaves 10-20mm, paired on stem, stalkless, elliptical or narrowly oblong with fine, translucent dots as though pierced by a pin. Flowers June–September. Flowers 17-25mm, hermaphrodite, in widely branched heads; 5 spear-shaped sepals shorter than petals; 5 wedge-shaped petals yellow with black dots at edge; with many stamens like a pin-cushion and 3 stigmas. Fruit 6mm, a pear-shaped capsule, splitting to release numerous oblong, pitted seeds, 1mm long. Grows in grassy places, hedges and open woods.

Common Dog-violet *Viola riviniana* An attractive hedgerow perennial with rather low-growing stems, 2-40cm long. Leaves 5-80mm, on alternate sides of stem, heart-shaped, slightly pointed, with rounded teeth, long-stalked. Flowers April–June. Flower 14-22mm, hermaphrodite, long-stalked, scentless; 5 sepals spear-shaped and shorter than the petals; 5 oval, overlapping petals blue-violet, unequal, the lower with a backward-pointing spur 3-5mm long; with 5 stamens and 1 stigma. Fruit 6-13mm, a 3-angled, pointed capsule, splitting to release numerous egg-shaped seeds, each 2-2.5mm. Grows in woods, hedges, heaths or amongst rocks.

Field Pansy *Viola arvensis* This relative of cultivated pansies has branched, nearly upright stems 15-40cm tall. Leaves 20-50mm, on alternate sides of stem between paired, leaf-like stipules, oblong or almost spoon-shaped with rounded teeth. Flowers April–October. Flowers 8-20mm, hermaphrodite; 5 sepals spear-shaped, sometimes longer than petals; 5 flattish, oval petals cream or yellow, sometimes tinged bluish-violet, unequal, side petals angled upwards and lowest spurred; with 5 stamens and 1 stigma. Fruit 6-8mm, a 3-angled, pointed capsule, splitting to eject many egg-shaped seeds, each 1.5mm. Grows in cultivated and waste ground.

Loosestrifes/Willowherbs

Purple-loosestrife *Lythrum salicaria* A tall, slender perennial with upright, 4-angled stems 60-120cm tall. Leaves 40-70mm, paired or in threes, spear-shaped or oval, pointed, with a heart-shaped, stalkless base. Flowers June–August. Long spikes of reddish-purple flowers are a distinctive feature with flowers often in rings. Flowers 10-15mm, hermaphrodite, short-stalked; 6 sepals joined into a tube; 6 nearly oval petals; with 12 stamens and 1 stigma. Fruit 3-4mm, an egg-shaped capsule, which splits to release many flattened seeds, each 1mm. Grows on margins of lakes, rivers or fens. Absent from parts of north.

Enchanter's-nightshade *Circaea lutetiana* An easily overlooked, very slender perennial of shady places, with upright stems 20-70cm tall. Leaves 40-100mm, paired on stem, oval, pointed, toothed, with base rounded and short-stalked. Flowers June–August. Flowers 4-8mm, hermaphrodite, rather insignificant, in a loose spike at tip of stem, with short stalk bent downwards in fruit; both sepals have bases joined into a short tube; 2 petals are deeply notched; with 2 stamens and a 2-lobed stigma. Fruit 3-4mm, egg-shaped with hooked bristles that cling to clothing or fur; with 1-2 seeds, each 2-2.5mm. Grows in woods, hedges and scrub. Absent from parts of north.

Rosebay Willowherb
Chamerion angustifolium Forming
extensive clumps, this
perennial sends up many
straight stems 30-120cm.
Leaves 50-150mm, spirally
arranged in contrast to other
willowherbs, spear-shaped or
elliptical, wavy and sometimes
toothed. Flowers July–
September. Flowers 20-30mm
hermaphrodite, in slender
spikes; 4 sepals purple; 4 oval,
notched petals pinkish-purple,
slightly unequal with the
upper two broadest; with 8
stamens and a 4-lobed stigma.
Fruit 25-80mm, slender, a
4-angled capsule, splitting to
release fluffy masses of egg-
shaped, plumed seeds, each
1-2mm. Grows in woodland
clearings, rocky places or
waste ground, often after fires.

Broad-leaved Willowherb
Epilobium montanum Spreading
by pink, scaly, creeping stems,
this perennial sends up
flowering stems 10-80cm tall.
Leaves 40-80mm, oval, pointed,
mostly paired but sometimes
in threes. Flowers June–
August. Flowers 6-10mm,
hermaphrodite, in elongated,
leafy head; 4 sepals often
reddish and shorter than the
petals; 4 petals purplish-pink,
narrowly oval, deeply
notched, equal; with 8
stamens and a 4-lobed stigma
on a long style. The 4-angled
capsule, 40-80mm long, splits
to release masses of plumed
egg-shaped, reddish-brown
seeds, each 1-1.2mm long.
Grows in woods, hedges,
amongst rocks or on
cultivated ground.

Ivy *Hedera helix* An evergreen climber with woody stems up to 30m tall and 25cm wide, anchored by clinging roots. Leaves are glossy, dark green, short-stalked and on alternate sides of stem; lower leaves 40-100mm with 3-5 radiating, triangular lobes; leaves on flowering stems oval or diamond-shaped. Flowers September–November. Flowers 5-8mm, hermaphrodite, rather insignificant, form compact, stalked heads; 5 sepals are tiny; 5 petals dull yellow, oval or nearly triangular; with 5 stamens and 1 stigma. Fruit 6-8mm, blackish, globular, rather leathery and berry-like, enclosing 2-5 whitish, papery-coated seeds. Grows in woods, hedges, rocks and walls.

Sea-holly *Eryngium maritimum* Pale blue and waxy, this perennial has thick, branched, hollow stems 15-60cm tall. Leaves 40-120mm, from base or on alternate sides of stem, holly-like, leathery almost circular with spine-tipped lobes. Flowers July–August. Flowers 6-8mm, hermaphrodite, in rather thistle-like, nearly globular, stalked heads; 5 spear-shaped sepals are spine-tipped; 5 narrow petals pale blue or whitish with notched tip; with 5 stamens and 2 stigmas. Fruit 5-6mm, egg-shaped, corky-walled, covered with hooked spines, splits into two, both halves retaining their seed. Grows on sand-dunes and shingle banks. Absent from parts of north.

Cow Parsley *Anthriscus sylvestris*
Forming billowing mounds of
white along roadsides, this
biennial or perennial has
upright, furrowed, hollow
stems 60-100cm tall. Leaves up
to 300mm, from base or
spirally arranged on stem,
fern-like, stalked, finely cut
into oval, toothed segments
15-25mm long. Flowers April–
June. Flowers 3-5mm,
hermaphrodite, in umbrella-
shaped heads, 20-60mm across,
with 4-10 main branches; 5
sepals are tiny; 5 notched
petals 1-2.5mm white, unequal
on outer flowers; with 5
stamens and 2 stigmas. Fruit
5-10mm, tapered, smooth,
blackish-brown, splitting into
two, with each half retaining
its seed. Grows in hedges,
wood margins and on walls.

Ground-elder *Aegopodium
podagraria* Spreading rapidly by
underground, creeping stems,
this perennial sends up many
grooved, upright, hollow
stems 40-100cm tall. Leaves
100-200mm, on alternate sides
of stem, divided into oval,
pointed, toothed segments
40-80mm long; lower leaves
have long, 3-angled stalks,
upper leaves have a broad base.
Flowers May–July. Flowers
1-3mm, hermaphrodite, in
umbrella-shaped heads,
20-60mm wide, with 15-20
branches; no sepals; 5 petals,
white with tip curved in; with
5 stamens and 2 stigmas. Fruit
3-4mm, egg-shaped, slightly
flattened, ridged, splitting into
two, with each half retaining
its seed. Grows on cultivated
or waste ground.

Carrots

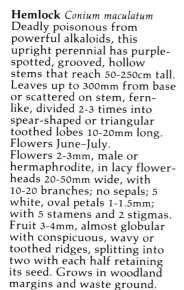

Hemlock *Conium maculatum*
Deadly poisonous from powerful alkaloids, this upright perennial has purple-spotted, grooved, hollow stems that reach 50-250cm tall. Leaves up to 300mm from base or scattered on stem, fern-like, divided 2-3 times into spear-shaped or triangular toothed lobes 10-20mm long. Flowers June–July. Flowers 2-3mm, male or hermaphrodite, in lacy flower-heads 20-50mm wide, with 10-20 branches; no sepals; 5 white, oval petals 1-1.5mm; with 5 stamens and 2 stigmas. Fruit 3-4mm, almost globular with conspicuous, wavy or toothed ridges, splitting into two with each half retaining its seed. Grows in woodland margins and waste ground.

Hogweed *Heracleum sphondylium*
Coarse and bristly, this upright biennial has stout, ridged, hollow stems 50-200cm tall. Leaves 150-600mm, from base or scattered on stem, with paired, lobed leaflets cut into oval or spear-shaped, toothed segments. Flowers June–September. Flowers 5-10mm, hermaphrodite, in plate-like flower-heads up to 15cm wide, with 7-25 branches; 5 sepals small and unequal; 5 petals 2-7mm, white or pink, notched; with 5 stamens and 2 stigmas. Fruit 7-8mm, flattened and nearly circular, ridged with dark lines, splitting into two with each half retaining its seed. Grows in grassy places, hedges or woods.

Upright Hedge-parsley *Torilis japonica* This annual, with upright, solid stems 5-125cm tall, is one of the last hedgerow species of the carrot family to flower. Leaves on alternate sides of the stem; divided into oval or spear-shaped, lobed or toothed, leaflets 10-20mm long. Flowers July–August. Flowers 2-3mm, hermaphrodite, in lacy, umbrella-shaped heads 15-40mm wide, with 5-12 branches; 5 small sepals are triangular; 5 unequal petals pink or purplish, notched; with 5 stamens and 2 stigmas. Fruit 3-4mm, egg-shaped, ridged, covered with spines, splitting into two, with each half retaining its seed. Grows in hedges and grassy places. Not common in extreme north.

Wild Carrot *Daucus carota* Smelling of fresh carrots, this bristly, upright biennial grows 30-100cm tall with ridged, solid stems. Leaves 4-7mm, on alternate sides of stem, divided into slender, lobed leaflets. Flowers June–August. Flowers 2-4mm, hermaphrodite, in umbrella-shaped heads 30-70mm wide, with many branches, a central flower is usually purple or red; 5 sepals tiny; 5 petals 1-2mm, white, notched; with 5 stamens and 2 stigmas. Fruit 2.5-4mm, spinily ridged 2.5-4mm, nearly oblong, splitting into two with each half retaining its seed; many fruits together in fruiting head. Grows in grassy places.

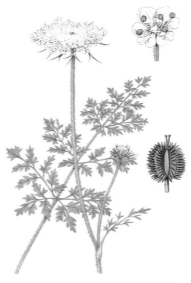

Heather *Calluna vulgaris*
Covering entire
mountainsides, this wiry little
evergreen has twisted woody
stems which root below and
angle upwards to 60cm or
more. Leaves 1-2mm, paired, in
four rows, closely packed,
pointed, slender, turned under
at the edge and with 2 small
projections at base. Flowers
July–September. Flowers 3-
4.5mm, hermaphrodite, in
narrow, often branched heads
30-150mm long; 4 oval or
oblong, pointed, purple sepals
are longer than petals and
joined below; 4 petals join
forming a bell; with 8 stamens
and 1 stigma. The capsule is
2-2.5mm long and splits to
release a few tiny seeds.
Grows on heaths, moors, bogs
or woodland edges.

Scarlet Pimpernel *Anagallis
arvensis* This common and
often weedy annual has
4-angled stems which are low-
growing or angle upwards
6-30cm or more. Leaves
15-18mm, paired oval or spear-
shaped, marked with tiny
black dots below. Flowers
June–August. Flowers 5-14mm,
hermaphrodite, do not last
long, on a long stalk which
curves back in fruit; 5 sepals
narrow and pointed; 5 oval
petals red (or rarely blue or
purple), equal and joined
below; with 5 stamens and 1
stigma. Fruit 2.5-4mm, a
globular capsule, opening by a
split that detaches the top,
releasing 12-45 circular seeds,
each 1-1.5mm. Grows on
cultivated and waste ground
or dunes.

Cowslip *Primula veris* From a very short, mostly undergound stem, this perennial produces a leafy tuft and upright, leafless stalks to the flower-heads, which reach 10-30cm tall. Leaves 50-200mm forming a rosette, oval or oblong, with small, rounded teeth. Flowers April–May. Flowers 10-15mm, hermaphrodite, form a stalked, usually one-sided, cluster of up to 30 flowers, nodding; 5 sepals form a tube with triangular lobes; 5 petals deep yellow, spotted orange at base, form a tube; with 5 stamens and 1 stigma. The egg-shaped capsule is 9-10mm long and opens to release many small, angular seeds. Grows in grassy places. Rare or absent from north.

Primrose *Primula vulgaris* Early to flower, this low-growing perennial has very short stems with a leafy tuft from which arise the stalked flowers. Leaves 80-200mm oval or rather spoon-shaped, toothed. Flowers December–May. Flowers 20-40mm, hermaphodite, clustered on a very short stem but each seems to grow on its own slender stalk; 5 sepals join to form a tube; 5 petals pale yellow or rarely pink, tubular below, with widely spreading, notched lobes; with 5 stamens and 1 stigma. Fruit 5-7mm, an almost globular capsule, opening to release numerous angular seeds, each 0.8-1mm. Grows in woods, hedges or grassy banks. Absent from parts of extreme north.

Thrift *Armeria maritima*
Forming grass-like tufts near
the sea, this perennial has
very short, stout stems and
long, unbranched stalks to the
flower-heads, which reach
5-30cm tall. Leaves 20-150mm,
slender, stalkless, forming a
rosette at base. Flowers April–
October. Flowers 7-10mm,
hermaphrodite, in rounded
clusters at tip of long stalk,
slightly scented; 5 sepals form
a papery funnel with 5 hairy
ribs; 5 equal, oval pink petals
are joined below; with 5
stamens and 5 stigmas. Fruit
2.5-3mm, a small, oblong
capsule surrounded by
remains of the flower,
opening to release an egg-
shaped seed 2-2.5mm long.
Grows on cliffs, rocks and
salt-marshes.

Common Centaury *Centaurium
erythraea* A slender annual or
biennial with one or a few
upright stems, 2-50cm tall and
branched above. Shiny, oval
or elliptical leaves 10-50mm
long form a rosette at base
and are paired on stem; upper
leaves smaller. Flowers June–
October. Flowers 10-14mm,
hermaphrodite, in flattish-
topped, widely branched
heads; 5 narrow, pointed
sepals are joined at base; 5
equal petals glossy pink or
rarely white, form tube below;
with 5 stamens and 2 stigmas.
The slender, pointed capsule is
8-12mm, opening to release
many rounded seeds, each 0.8-
1mm. Grows in dry, sunny,
grassy places and dunes.
Absent from extreme north.

Lady's Bedstraw *Galium verum*
Scented like new-mown hay,
this slender perennial has
4-angled, much-branched
stems which angle upwards
15-100cm, often sprawling
over neighbouring plants.
Leaves 6-25mm, in distinctive
rings of 8-12, stalkless, needle-
like. Flowers July–August.
Flowers 2-4mm,
hermaphrodite, forming
branched clusters at tip of
stems, 4 sepals are tiny; 4
petals 1-2mm, golden yellow,
oval, widely-spreading, joined
below forming a short tube;
with 4 stamens and 2 stigmas.
Small black, smooth 2-lobed
fruit splits into two with each
half retaining its seed. Grows
in grassy places and dunes.

Cleavers *Galium aparine*
Clinging tenaciously to animal
fur or clothing, this annual
has trailing or clambering,
4-angled stems 15-120cm tall,
with stiff, hook-like hairs.
Leaves 12-50mm, encircle stem
in rings of 6-8, bristly,
stalkless, spear-shaped or
elliptical. Flowers June–
August. Flowers 1.5-2mm,
hermaphrodite, rather
insignificant, 2-5 flowers
grouped in branched heads; 4
tiny sepals; 4 oval, widely
spreading, white petals
0.6-1mm, the bases joined into
a short tube; with 4 stamens
and 2 stigmas. Fruit 4-6mm,
covered with whitish, hooked
bristles, splits in two, with
each half retaining its seed.
Grows in hedges, on waste
ground or amongst rocks.

Bindweeds

Hedge Bindweed *Calystegia sepium* This rampant vine reaches 3m tall with stems that twine anti-clockwise; also spreading underground to make new plants. Leaves up to 150mm, spirally arranged on stem, heart-shaped or angular. Flowers April–July. Spectacular flowers 30-55mm, hermaphrodite, funnels of purest white; 5 sepals 10-12mm, oval and almost hidden by 2 broad bracts; 5 equal petals almost completely joined; with 5 stamens and 2 stigmas. A globular capsule 7-12mm long, the fruit splits to release 4 angular, brown seeds, each 4-7mm. Grows in hedges and woods or on waste and cultivated ground. Absent from parts of extreme north.

Field Bindweed *Convolvulus arvensis* A perennial climber twining anti-clockwise up to 1m or creeping over bare ground and spreading underground to make new plants. Leaves 20-50mm, spirally arranged on stem, arrow-shaped or oval. Flowers June–September. Flowers 10-30mm, hermaphrodite, scented, pleated, funnel-shaped, solitary or in small clusters; 5 small sepals joined at base; 5 pastel pink and white petals almost completely joined; with 5 stamens and 2 stigmas. Fruit 3-5mm, an almost globular capsule, opening to release 2-4 angular, rough seeds, each 2.5-4mm. Grows on cultivated or waste ground and on coasts.

Bugloss *Anchusa arvensis* This very bristly annual has upright stems 15-60cm tall. Leaves 30-150mm, on alternate sides of stem, spear-shaped or oblong, with wavy, toothed edge; base of upper leaves partly clasps stem. Flowers June–September. Flowers 4-6mm, hermaphrodite, in long heads coiled at the tip; 5 sepals 4-5mm, spear-shaped; 5 bright-blue petals form a curved tube at base, with a ring of white scales at the mouth; with 5 stamens and 1 stigma. The fruit splits into four egg-shaped, nut-like segments, each 3-4mm and retaining its seed. Grows in arable fields, heaths or near the sea. Absent from parts of extreme north.

Field Forget-me-not *Myosotis arvensis* This spring-flowering, rather hairy biennial has upright, branched stems 15-30cm, or rarely 60cm, tall. Leaves 6-80mm, form a rosette or on alternate sides of stem, oblong or spear-shaped. Flowers April–September. Flowers 3-5mm, hermaphrodite, pink buds open as blue, yellow-eyed flowers in slender heads which gradually uncoil; 5 sepals, joined by their bases, are covered in hooked hairs; 5 petals form a very short tube; with 5 stamens and 1 stigma. The fruit splits into four egg-shaped, angular, nut-like parts, each 1.5-2mm, glossy brown and retaining its seed. Grows in woods, hedges, cultivated ground or dunes.

Common Comfrey *Symphytum officinale* Robust and bristly, this upright perennial is usually found near water and has branched, winged stems 30-120cm tall. Leaves 40-250mm, on alternate sides of stem, oval or spear-shaped; only lower leaves have stalks. Flowers May–June. Flowers 15-18mm, hermaphodite, in curved heads; 5 pointed sepals form a narrow tube, much shorter than the petals; 5 equal petals yellowish-white flushed with red, purple or pink, forming a tube; with 5 stamens and 1 stigma. Four nut-like, egg-shaped segments of the fruit are 5-6mm, glossy black, each retaining its seed. Grows in grassy places or river-banks.

Wood Sage *Teucrium scorodonia* A woody-based, upright perennial, with branched stems 15-50cm tall. Leaves 30-70mm, paired either side of stem, crinkly, grey-green, oval edged with rounded teeth. Flowers July–September. Flowers 9-12mm, hermaphrodite, in long spikes from tip of stem; 5 sepals 4-6mm, joined except for pointed teeth, usually with upper tooth largest; 5 petals greenish-yellow, joined into a narrow tube; with 4 stamens and a forked style bearing 2 stigmas. The fruit splits into four nut-like parts, each 1.5-2mm, egg-shaped, smooth retaining its seed. Grows on heaths, dunes or bordering woodland, mostly on dry soils. Absent from parts of north.

Bugle *Ajuga reptans* Often grown in gardens, this perennial creeps over the ground with 4-angled, rooting stems and sends up flowering stems 10-40cm tall. Leaves 25-90mm, lower leaves form a rosette but stem-leaves are paired; each leaf blunt and sometimes toothed, often stalked. Flowers May–July. Flowers 14-17mm, hermaphrodite, blue, contrasting with blackish-violet bracts, 6 flowers form a loose spike; 5 sepals form a tube with nearly equal teeth; 5 petals form a tube with three prominent lower lobes; with 4 stamens and 2 stigmas. The fruit splits into four nut-like parts, each egg-shaped with a net-like pattern. Grows in woods and grassy places.

Selfheal *Prunella vulgaris* Compact in close-grazed turf, this perennial has flowering stems angled upwards 5-50cm tall. Leaves 20-50mm, paired on stem, oval or diamond-shaped. Flowers June–September. Flowers 10-15mm, hermaphrodite, clusters of 6 flowers form short, oblong flower-heads; 5 sepals form a tube with lower two teeth longer; 5 violet petals form a tube with two upper lobes joined and hood-like, the lower three bent back; with 4 stamens and 2 stigmas. Splitting into four nut-like parts, the fruit has smooth, oblong segments 2-2.5mm long, each retaining its seed. Grows in grassland or woodland clearings.

Mints

Common Hemp-nettle
Galeopsis tetrahit Distinctively
swollen below each leaf, the
4-angled, nearly upright stems
of this bristly annual are
10-100cm tall. Leaves
25-100mm, paired on stem,
nettle-like, oval, pointed,
sharply toothed. Flowers July–
September. Flowers 15-28mm,
hermaphrodite, form clusters
at leaf-bases near the tip of
stem; 5 sepals form a tube
with spine-tipped teeth; 5
petals purple or pinkish,
striped and spotted with
deeper purple, join in a tube
with hood-like upper lobes,
the lower three bent back;
with 4 stamens and 2 stigmas.
The fruit splits into four nut-
like parts, each retaining its
seed. Grows in cultivated
ground, hedges or woods.

Hedge Woundwort *Stachys
sylvatica* Strong-smelling, this
rather hairy perennial has
upright, branched stems
30-120cm tall. Leaves
40-140mm, paired on stem,
oval or heart-shaped, pointed,
coarsely toothed. Flowers
July–August. Flowers
13-18mm, hermaphrodite, in
small groups clustered into
elongated heads; 5 sepals form
a hairy tube with triangular
teeth; 5 petals reddish-purple,
joined below, with upper two
lobes hood-like and lower
three bent back; with 4
stamens and 2 stigmas. The
fruit splits into four nut-like
parts, each egg-shaped with a
rounded tip and retaining its
seed. Grows in woods, hedges
or other shady places.

White Dead-nettle *Lamium album* A softly hairy perennial with upright stems 20-80cm tall. Leaves 25-120mm, paired on stem, nettle-like, oval, pointed, coarsely toothed. Flowers May–December. Flowers 20-25mm, hermaphrodite, clustered at base of upper leaves; 5 sepals joined except for slender, pointed teeth; 5 white petals join to form narrow tube with upper two lobes hood-like and lower lobes bent back; with 4 stamens and 2 stigmas. The fruit splits into four nut-like parts, each 2.5-3mm and retaining its seed. Grows in hedges, along roadsides and on waste ground.

Red Dead-nettle *Lamium purpureum* Four-angled, creeping, rooting stems of this annual turn upright to flower, reaching 10-45cm tall. Leaves 10-50mm, paired on stem, sometimes purple-tinged, oval, with rounded teeth. Flowers March–October. Flowers 10-18mm, hermaphrodite, forming clusters at base of upper leaves; 5 sepals joined except for long teeth; 5 pinkish-purple petals joined into a tube with upper two lobes hood-like, lower lobes divided and toothed; with 4 stamens and 2 stigmas. The fruit splits into four nut-like parts, each 2-2.5mm and retaining its seed. Grows on cultivated and waste ground.

Mints

Ground-ivy *Glechoma hederacea*
Creeping beneath hedges and over woodland floors, this perennial has rooting stems 10-50cm long that turn upwards to flower. Leaves 5-35mm, paired on stem, kidney-shaped to oval, hairy, coarsely toothed. Flowers March–May. Flowers 15-22mm, either female or hermaphrodite, paired or in groups of four at leaf-base; 5 sepals joined except for teeth; 5 petals bluish-violet, joined into a tube below, upper two lobes hood-like, lower three larger; with 4 stamens and 2 stigmas. The fruit splits into four egg-shaped, nut-like parts, each 2-3mm, smooth and retaining its seed. Grows in bushy or wooded grassy places.

Wild Thyme *Thymus praecox* Its distinctive aroma pervading the air, this mat-forming perennial has long, creeping, rooting stems up to 8cm tall. Leaves 4-8mm, paired on stem, almost circular. Flowers May–August. Flowers 4-7mm female or hermaphrodite, in compact heads; 5 sepals form a tube, the upper three teeth short but the lower two long; 5 purple petals joined into a short tube below; with 4 stamens and 2 stigmas. The fruit splits into four nut-like parts, each 0.7-1mm, egg-shaped, smooth, retaining its seed. Grows in grassy places, heaths, dunes or amongst rocks. Absent from much of north.

Water Mint *Mentha aquatica*
With its own distinctive
aroma, this relative of the
garden mint is a perennial
with 4-angled stems reaching
15-90cm tall. Leaves 20-90mm,
paired on stem, oval, hairy,
toothed. Flowers July–
October. Flowers 5-8mm,
hermaphrodite, forming
rounded, short-stalked
clusters near the top of stem;
5 sepals form a tube with
pointed teeth; 5 pinkish-lilac
petals join to form short tube
at base, lower three lobes
slightly larger; with 4 stamens
and 2 stigmas. The fruit splits
into four nut-like parts, each
1-1.5mm, egg-shaped, pale
brown and retains its seed.
Grows in woods, marshes and
by rivers.

Bittersweet *Solanum dulcamara*
Woody below, stems of this
perennial trail or clamber over
other plants, reaching
30-200cm tall. Leaves 30-90mm,
mostly on alternate sides of
stem, lobed or oval, pointed.
Flowers June–September.
Flowers 10-15mm,
hermaphodite, in widely
branched clusters of 10-25; 5
short sepals form a tube with
short teeth; 5 purple petals
4-7mm, joined below, with
spear-shaped lobes curved
back; with 5 yellow stamens
and 1 stigma. Poisonous,
glossy red, egg-shaped berries
are 10-15mm, each containing
several rounded, flattened
seeds 1.7-2mm wide. Grows in
hedges, woods, amongst rocks
and shingle or on waste
ground.

Great Mullein *Verbascum thapsus* Poker-straight, the whitish-woolly stems of this biennial grow 30-200cm tall. Leaves 40-500mm, first-year leaves form a rosette but later leaves spiral around stem, oval to oblong. Flowers June–August. Flowers 12-30mm, hermaphrodite, in a dense spike; 5 oval, pointed sepals joined at base; 5 yellow, rounded petals joined below; with 5 stamens and 1 stigma. An egg-shaped capsule, the fruit is 7-10mm, splitting to release numerous oblong, pitted seeds, each 0.8-1mm. Grows on grassy banks and waste ground. Absent from parts of north.

Common Figwort *Scrophularia nodosa* With upright, 4-angled, branched stems, this perennial grows 30-80cm tall. Leaves 60-130mm, paired on stem, oval, dark green, unevenly toothed. Flowers June–September. Flowers 7-10mm, hermaphrodite, globular, 5-7 flowers, form branched heads; 5 short, oval sepals have papery edges and joined bases; 5 dull reddish-brown and green petals are joined except for rounded lobes with upper two longer than the lower; with 4 stamens and 1 swollen stigma. The fruit is an egg-shaped capsule, 5-10mm long, splitting to release many oblong, pitted seeds, each 0.8-1mm. Grows in woods and hedges.

Foxglove *Digitalis purpurea* This biennial or perennial has robust, upright, unbranched stems 50-150cm tall. Leaves 150-300mm, lower leaves form a rosette while others spiral around stem, oval or spear-shaped with rounded teeth. Flowers June–September. Flowers 40-50mm hermaphrodite, in slender spires, tubular, purple, usually spotted inside with purple ringed by white; 5 short, oval sepals joined below; 5 petals 40-50mm, almost completely joined into a flared tube; with 4 stamens and a forked stigma. The egg-shaped capsule, 14-18mm, splits releasing many oblong, pitted seeds, each 0.8-1mm. Grows in woodland clearings, heaths or rocky places.

Common Field-speedwell *Veronica persica* Introduced from Asia, this low growing annual has branched stems angling upwards 10-40cm tall. Leaves 10-30mm, on alternate sides of stem or paired below, oval, blunt, coarsely toothed. Flowers January–December. Attractive sky-blue and white flowers are 8-12mm, hermaphrodite; 4 oval sepals nearly equal the petals; 4 unequal petals joined at base, falling together soon after opening; with 2 stamens and 1 stigma. Fruit 5-10mm, is a nodding, two-lobed capsule, flattened, splitting to release a few oblong seeds, each 1.5-1.8mm. Usually a weed of arable fields and gardens.

Figworts

Common Toadflax *Linaria vulgaris* An upright perennial, with many stems budding from creeping roots and reaching 30-80cm tall. Leaves 20-60mm, mostly spirally arranged on stem, slender, pointed. Flowers July–October. Snapdragon-like flowers 20-33mm, hermaphrodite, in slender spikes, hinge open to admit insect visitors; 5 oval, short sepals joined below; 5 petals joined into a tube with a spur at the base; with 4 stamens and 1 stigma. An oblong capsule, the fruit is 5-11mm long and opens by two pores to release many circular, flattened seeds, each 2-3mm and black. Grows in grassy and waste places.

Yellow-rattle *Rhinanthus minor* An unusual, partly parasitic annual, with upright, often black-spotted stems 12-50cm tall. Leaves 10-50mm, paired on stem, oblong, toothed. Flowers May–August. Flowers 12-15mm, hermaphrodite in oblong spikes at the tip of stems; 4 sepals are joined, becoming enlarged and papery in fruit; 5 yellow or purple-tinged petals joined into a tube, the upper two lobes hood-like; with 4 stamens and 1 stigma. Fruit 10-12mm, a rounded, flattened capsule, which rattles until it splits to release the few flattened, circular seeds, each 4-5mm. Grows in grassland and marshes, especially in hills or mountains.

Red Bartsia *Odontites verna*
A partial parasite feeding on
roots of neighbouring plants,
this annual has angular,
upright stems 10-50cm tall.
Leaves 12-40mm, paired on
stem, spear-shaped, pointed,
with few teeth. Flowers July–
September. Flowers 8-10mm,
hermaphrodite, in slender,
rather loose spikes 30-100mm
long; 4 sepals join to form a
tube with pointed teeth; 5
purplish-pink petals form a
tube, with two upper lobes
hood-like, the three lower
lobes longer; with 4
protruding stamens and 1
stigma. The oblong, hairy
capsule, 6-8mm long, splits to
release many grooved seeds,
each 1-2mm. Grows in grassy
places, roadsides, arable fields
and waste land.

Marsh Lousewort *Pedicularis
palustris* Sometimes tinged
purple, this partly parasitic
annual or biennial has a stout,
rather succulent stem 8-60cm
tall. Leaves 20-40mm, on
alternate sides of stem, deeply
cut into many paired, toothed
lobes. Flowers May–
September. Flowers 18-25mm,
hermaphrodite, clustered in a
spike; 5 sepals joined into a
hairy tube, the tube becoming
swollen in fruit; 5 purplish-
pink petals fused below with
upper two lobes joined and
hood-like, bearing two teeth
on each side; with 4 stamens
and 1 stigma. Curved and
flattened, the capsule is
10-12mm, opening to release a
few oblong seeds, each 2-3mm.
Grows in meadows, damp
heaths and other wet places.

Broomrapes/Bladderworts

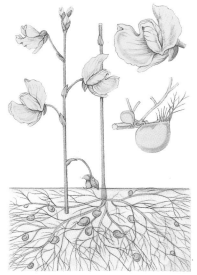

Greater Broomrape *Orobanche rapum-genistae* Sickly yellow or red-tinged, this curious perennial is a parasite of gorse and broom, with a sticky stem 20-80cm tall. Leaves 15-25mm, spirally arranged on stem, scale-like, oval or spear-shaped. Flowers May–July. Flowers 20-25mm, hermaphrodite, in a long, crowded spike; 4 sepals joined in a tube; 5 pale yellow petals form a curved tube with lower three lobes bent downwards and the upper two short; with 4 stamens and 1 stigma. Fruit 10-14mm, an oblong capsule, splitting to release myriads of dust-like seeds, each 0.3mm. Grows in heaths or woodland clearings. Mainly in south.

Greater Bladderwort
Utricularia vulgaris
A remarkable carnivorous aquatic plant with submerged, leafy stems up to 1m and leafless flowering stems rising 10-20cm above the water. Leaves 20-25mm, spirally arranged on stem, hair-like, some have bladders up to 3mm long, springing open to trap and digest aquatic animals. Flowers July–August. Flowers 12-18mm, hermaphrodite, in a spike-like head; 2 oval sepals join below; 2 deep yellow petals joined into a tube with spur at base; with 2 stamens and a 2-lobed stigma. The globular capsule, 3-5mm, splits to release many angular seeds, each 0.5-0.7mm. Grows in ponds, lakes or ditches.

Greater Plantain *Plantago major*
A familiar weed of lawns, this perennial makes a tough, leafy rosette and sends up stalked flowering spikes about 15cm or more tall. Leaves 100-300mm, oval or elliptical, sometimes toothed. Flowers May–September. Flowers 2-3mm, hermaphrodite, rather insignificant, forming a long slender spike; 4 oval, brownish, papery sepals are shorter than petals; 4 yellowish-white petals form a tube beneath oval lobes; with 4 long, protruding stamens and 1 stigma. Fruit 2-4mm, oblong capsule, top detaches to release 6-13 elliptical, flattened seeds, each 1-1.5mm. Grows in grassy places and cultivated or waste ground.

Ribwort *Plantago lanceolata*
A familiar wayside plant, this perennial forms a tuft of long, slender leaves and sends up long-stalked flower-heads reaching 10-45cm tall. Leaves 100-300mm, spear-shaped, sometimes toothed, with 3-5 almost parallel veins. Flowers April–August. Flowers 3-5mm, hermaphrodite, crowded on flower-head 10-20mm long, at top of very long stalk, 4 papery sepals are joined below; 4 brownish petals form a tube beneath oval lobes; with 4 long, protruding stamens and 1 stigma. Fruit 3-5mm, an oblong capsule; top detaches to release 2 elliptical, flattened seeds, each 2-3mm. Grows in grassy places.

Honeysuckle *Lonicera periclymenum* Long, woody stems of this climber twine clockwise up to 6m tall or trail on the ground. Leaves 30-70mm, paired on stem, bluish-green, oval or oblong, pointed. Flowers June–September. Flowers 40-50mm, hermaphrodite, richly scented, creamy-white suffused with red or purple, in heads containing 4-30 flowers; 5 sepals 2-5mm joined at base; petals form slender, flared trumpet with upper four lobes joined into a broad lip and the lower curved back; with 5 stamens and 1 stigma. Clusters of crimson berries are each 7-10mm, globular, containing a few oblong seeds 4-5mm long. Grows in woods, hedges or amongst rocks.

Moschatel *Adoxa moschatellina* Easily overlooked, this curious little perennial has upright, unbranched stems 5-10cm tall. Leaves 8-30mm, from base or 2-3 together on stem, fern-like, pale green, divided into three leaflets. Flowers April–May. Flowers 6-8mm, hermaphrodite, one flower faces upwards and four face outwards; 2 or 3 oval sepals are 1.5-2mm long; 4 or 5 oval, yellowish-green petals joined at base; with 4 or 5 stamens and 4 or 5 stigmas. In a compact head, the greenish, berry-like fruits are 3-5mm, each containing 3-5 oval, flattened seeds 2-3mm long. Grows in woods, hedges or amongst rocks.

Teasel *Dipsacus fullonum*
A robust, prickly biennial, with
upright, branched stems up to
2m tall. Leaves up to 400mm,
first year leaves form a
rosette, others paired on stem
with broad bases forming a
cup that fills with rain-water,
oblong, elliptical or spear-
shaped, sometimes toothed.
Flowers July–August. Flowers
8-12mm, hermaphrodite, in
very spiny, oblong or conical
flower-heads, 30-80mm long;
tiny sepals form a cup-shaped
rim; 4 rosy purple petals
joined into a tube; with 2-4
stamens and 1 stigma. Each
flower produces a nut-like,
oblong, 4-angled fruit 4-5mm
long, which retains its seed.
Grows in grassy places.

Field Scabious *Knautia arvensis*
This pastel-flowered meadow
beauty is a perennial with
branched, upright stems
25-100cm tall. Leaves up to
300mm, forming a rosette or
paired on stem, hairy, divided
into paired, often toothed,
lobes. Flowers July–
September. Broad, bluish-lilac,
flower-heads, 30-40mm wide,
consist of numerous female or
hermaphrodite flowers,
larger, outer flowers up to
14mm; 8 short sepals form
slender, hairy teeth; tube
formed by petals ends in
unequal lobes; with 4 pink
stamens and 1 stigma. Each
flower forms a nut-like,
cylindrical, hairy fruit, 5-6mm
long, which retains its seed.
Grows in grassy places.

Common Valerian *Valeriana officinalis* A tall perennial with flowering stems turning upright from a creeping base and reaching 20-150cm tall. Leaves 25-200mm, paired on stem, cut into spear-shaped, often toothed, paired leaflets. Flowers June–August. Flowers 4-5mm, hermaphrodite, in broad, branched heads at tip of stems; sepals form an inrolled ring, each becomes long and feathery in fruit; 5 pinkish-lilac petals form a tube with oblong, rounded lobes; with 3 stamens and a 3-lobed stigma. Each nut-like, oval, flattened fruit is 2.5-4mm, bearing a feathery parachute and retaining its seed. Grows in grassy places, fen or scrub.

Harebell *Campanula rotundifolia* A delicate, slender perennial 15-40cm tall with low-growing stems that turn upright to flower. Leaves alternate on stem, vary greatly; circular basal leaves 5-15mm, with rounded teeth and a stalk; longer upper leaves very narrow, parallel-sided and stalkless. Flowers July–September. Flowers 10-20mm, hermaphrodite, nodding, pale blue bells on long stalks; 5 slender sepals join with green, cupped base of flower; 5 petals end in broad, oval lobes; with 5 stamens and a 3-lobed stigma. Capsule 4-6mm, cone-shaped and nodding; opening by pores to release many oblong seeds, each 0.6-0.8mm. Grows in grassy places, heaths and dunes.

Daisy *Bellis perennis* This
perennial is often a weed of
lawns, with a leafy rosette
sending up leafless flowering
stalks 3-20cm tall. Leaves
20-40mm oval or spoon-
shaped, round-tipped,
toothed. Flowers March–
October. Familiar in daisy-
chains, flower-heads, each
16-25mm wide, have an
unusual structure; tiny,
yellow, hermaphrodite
flowers (florets) are
surrounded by whitish, strap-
shaped, female florets, with
oblong, sepal-like bracts 3-
5mm long; tiny sepals are hair-
like; 5 petals form a tube,
outer florets form long lobe;
with 5 stamens and 1 stigma.
Each floret produces a hairy,
oblong, nut-like fruit 1.5-2mm
long. Grows in short grass.

Sea Aster *Aster tripolium*
Forming large clumps in salt-
marshes, this upright
perennial has stout, branched
stems 15-100cm tall. Leaves 70-
120mm, spirally arranged on
stem, thick, succulent,
sometimes toothed. Flowers
July–October. Daisy-like
flower-heads of purple and
yellow are 8-20mm wide; each
formed by hermaphrodite
inner florets surrounded by
female outer florets, both
within sepal-like bracts; sepals
are hair-like; 5 petals form a
tube, outer florets form a long
lobe; with 5 stamens and 1
stigma. Nut-like fruits are
5-6mm with a long parachute.
Grows in salt-marshes, on
sea-cliffs or rocks.

Daisies

Goldenrod *Solidago virgaurea*
Blackish, upright stems of this
perennial grow 5-75cm, or
more, tall. Leaves 20-100mm,
spirally arranged on stem,
oval or elliptical, pointed,
toothed. Flowers July–
September. Golden, daisy-like
flower-heads, 8-20mm long,
consist of tiny hermaphrodite
flowers (florets) surrounded
by 6-12 female florets, both
within narrow, sepal-like
bracts; sepals are hair-like; 5
petals form a tube, outer
florets form long lobe; with 5
stamens and 1 stigma. Nut-
like and ribbed, the fruit is
3-4mm long and has a
parachute of hairs. Grows on
cliffs, amongst rocks, in
grassy places, woods or dunes.

Trifid Bur-marigold *Bidens
tripartita* This rather drab
water-side annual has upright,
stems 15-60cm, or rarely 1m
tall. Paired leaves, 50-150mm
long, are deeply cut into three
spear-shaped, toothed lobes.
Flowers July–September. Dull
yellow, daisy-like heads, 15-
25mm wide, consist of tiny
hermaphrodite flowers
(florets) separated by small
scales and surrounded by 2
rows of bracts; sepals are
bristle-like; 5 petals form a
tube; with 5 stamens and 1
stigma. The oblong, nut-like
fruit, 5-6mm long, is flattened
with 4 barbed angles tipped by
barbed bristles. Grows in
ponds, streams and damp
meadows.

Common Cudweed *Filago vulgaris* Woolly and whitish, this annual has upright stems 5-45cm tall. Leaves 10-30mm, spirally arranged on stem, spear-shaped. Flowers July–August. Yellowish, daisy-like flower-heads are 4-5mm wide, in compact clusters of 20-35; each consists of tiny yellow, hermaphrodite flowers (florets), surrounded by 20-25 female florets, both within sepal-like bracts; tiny sepals are hair-like; 5 equal petals form a tube; with 5 stamens joined and 1 stigma. The oblong, nut-like fruit, 0.6-0.7mm long, retains its seed; inner fruits have a parachute of hairs. Grows in grassy places, heaths or waste ground.

Mugwort *Artemisia vulgaris* A robust, rather sombre perennial, with grooved, reddish stems 60-120cm, or rarely 2m, tall. Leaves 50-80mm, spirally arranged on stem, deeply lobed and toothed, dark green above, silvery with dense hairs below. Flowers July–September. Reddish-brown, daisy-like flower-heads are 3-4mm long, each head formed by hermaphrodite flowers (florets) surrounded by female florets, both within sepal-like bracts 2.5-3mm long; no sepals; 5 equal petals form a tube; with 5 stamens and 1 stigma. Each floret produces a smooth, nut-like fruit 1-1.5mm long, which retains its seed. Grows on waste ground, roadsides and in hedges.

Daisies

Yarrow *Achillea millefolium*
With strong-smelling, rather woolly leaves, this perennial has upright, grooved stems 8-65cm tall. Leaves 50-160mm, arranged spirally on stem, feathery, finely divided into slender lobes. Flowers June–August. Flat-topped clusters of white or pink, daisy-like flower-heads are distinctive; each head 4-6mm wide, consists of tiny hermaphrodite flowers (florets) surrounded by larger female florets, both enclosed by bracts; no sepals; 5 petals form a tube; with 5 stamens and 1 stigma. The flattened, shiny, nut-like fruit is 1.5-2mm long and retains its seed. Grows in grassy places or hedges.

Tansy *Tanacetum vulgare*
Sometimes grown as a pot-herb, this robust, strong-smelling perennial has upright, angular stems 30-150cm tall. Leaves 150-250mm, arranged spirally on stem, deeply cut, dark green, with paired, pointed, toothed lobes. Flowers July–September. In flattish clusters, the deep yellow, button-like flower-heads are each 7-12mm wide; consist of tiny hermaphrodite flowers (florets) surrounded by larger female florets, both enclosed by bracts; sepals form a slight rim; 5 petals form a tube; with 5 stamens and 1 stigma. Each floret produces a 5-ribbed, nut-like fruit 1.5-1.8mm long, which retains its seed. Grows in hedges or on waste ground.

Scentless Mayweed
Tripleurospermum inodorum
Leaves without scent
distinguish this annual daisy
from similar cornfield species;
its upright, branched stems
are 15-80cm tall. Leaves
20-100mm, on alternate sides
of stem, finely divided into
long, slender segments.
Flowers July–September.
Daisy-like heads, each
15-45mm wide, formed by tiny
yellow, hermaphrodite,
flowers (florets), surrounded
by long, white, female florets
10-18mm long, both enclosed
by bracts; sepals form a tiny
rim; 5 petals form a tube; with
5 stamens and 1 stigma.
Oblong, 3-ribbed and nut-like,
the fruit is 2-3mm and retains
its seed. Grows in arable fields
or on waste ground.

Oxeye Daisy *Leucanthemum
vulgare* Brightening pasture,
roadside and railway
embankment, this attractive
perennial has unbranched,
upright stems 20-100cm tall.
Leaves 15-100mm, arranged
spirally on stem, oval or
oblong, toothed or lobed.
Flowers June–August.
Solitary, daisy-like heads
25-50mm wide consist of tiny
yellow, hermaphrodite
flowers (florets) surrounded
by long, white, female florets,
both enclosed by bracts; sepals
are scale-like or absent; 5
petals form a tube; with 5
stamens and 1 stigma. The
cylindrical or slightly
flattened, 5-10 ribbed, nut-like
fruit is 2-3mm, and retains its
seed. Grows in grassy places.

Daisies

Colt's-foot *Tussilago farfara*
This early-flowering perennial
forms clumps of scaly,
purplish, leafless flowering-
stems, 5-15cm tall, with leaves
growing later. Leaves
100-300mm, rounded or
angular with felt-like hairs
beneath; the heart-shaped
base has a long grooved stalk.
Flowers March–April. Bright
yellow, solitary, daisy-like
heads, 15-35mm wide, consist
of a few tiny male flowers
(florets) surrounded by many
strap-shaped female florets,
all bordered by bracts; sepals
are hair-like; 5 petals form a
tube; with 5 stamens and 1
stigma. The smooth, nut-like
fruit, 5-10mm long, has a
parachute of long hairs.
Grows on grassy banks and
river shingle.

Butterbur *Petasites hybridus*
Scaly, stout, leafless flowering
stems of this perennial are
10-80cm tall and grow before
leaves sprout from an
underground stem. Leaves
100-900mm, toothed, rhubarb-
like, felted below. Flowers
March–May. In a cluster of
20-40, the purplish-pink,
daisy-like heads consist of tiny
flowers (florets) within rows
of bracts; male heads, 7-12mm
wide, may have several female
florets; smaller female heads
include a few sterile florets;
sepals are hair-like; 5 petals
form a tube; with 5 stamens
and 1 stigma. The smooth,
nut-like fruit, 2-3mm long, has
a parachute of hairs. Grows
by running water.

Common Ragwort *Senecio
jacobaea* Often stripped by
cinnabar moth caterpillars,
this poisonous biennial or
perennial has upright stems
30-150cm tall. Leaves
25-200mm, from base or
spirally arranged, deeply cut
into toothed lobes. Flowers
June–October. Deep yellow,
daisy-like flower-heads are
15-25mm wide, each with tiny
hermaphrodite flowers
(florets) ringed by 12-15
female florets, all enclosed by
bracts; sepals are hair-like; 5
petals form a tube; with 5
stamens and 1 stigma. Nut-
like and 8-ribbed, each fruit is
1.5-2mm, retaining its seed;
inner fruits have a parachute
of hairs. Grows in grassy
places, on waste ground or
dunes.

Groundsel *Senecio vulgaris* Very
common annual with
succulent, branched and
sometimes cottony stems
8-45cm tall. Leaves 50-150mm,
on alternate sides of stem,
lobed, toothed, oblong.
Flowers January–December.
Dull yellow, cylindrical
flower-heads are 8-10mm long,
each with tiny hermaphrodite
flowers (florets), occasionally
surrounded by up to 12
elongated female florets, all
enclosed by bracts; sepals
form a ring of hairs; 5 petals
form a tube; with 5 stamens
and 1 stigma. Cylindrical with
hairy ribs, the fruit is 1.5-2mm,
with hairy parachute. Grows
on cultivated and waste
ground.

Daisies

Spear Thistle *Cirsium vulgare*
Spiny throughout, this biennial has upright, winged stems 30-150cm or rarely 3m, tall. Leaves 150-300mm, from base or spirally arranged on stem, spear-shaped with a very spiny edge, and cottony beneath. Flowers July–October. Handsome, reddish-purple thistle flowers in heads 30-50mm long, consist of tiny hermaphrodite or female flowers (florets) within several rows of bracts; tiny sepals are hair-like; 5 petals form a tube; with 5 stamens and 1 stigma. Each floret produces an oblong, nut-like fruit, 3.5-5mm long with feathery parachute 20-30mm long, which soon detaches. Grows in grassland, hedges or on waste ground.

Common Knapweed *Centaurea nigra* A tough, coarse perennial with upright, grooved stems 15-100cm tall. Roughly hairy leaves 50-250mm from base or spirally arranged on stem, oval to spear-shaped with a wavy edge. Flowers June–September. Each compact, rather solid, reddish-purple flower-head is 12-20mm, borne on swollen-tipped stalk and thistle-like, with tiny hermaphrodite flowers (florets) within rows of sepal-like bracts; sepals are hair-like; 5 petals form a tube; with 5 stamens and 1 stigma. The oblong, pale brown, nut-like fruit is 3-4mm long and bears a tuft of bristles. Grows in grassy places.

Lesser Burdock *Arctium minus*
A coarse biennial with
upright, grooved, branched
stems 60-130cm tall. Leaves
30-400mm, spirally arranged
on stem, oval or oblong,
usually toothed; lower leaves
with a long, hollow stalk,
upper leaves short-stalked.
Flowers July–September.
Globular, reddish-purple
flower-heads are 15-18mm
long and thistle-like, with tiny
hermaphrodite flowers
(florets) enclosed by bracts;
sepals are bristle-like; 5 petals
form a tube; with 5 stamens
and 1 stigma. Fruiting heads
are burs that stick to clothing
or animal fur, containing nut-
like, oblong, mottled fruits 5-
7mm long, each with a tuft of
bristles. Grows on waste
ground, in hedges and woods.

Smooth Sow-thistle *Sonchus
oleraceus* This weedy annual or
biennial has upright, 5-angled,
hollow stems 10-150cm tall,
exuding milky sap if broken.
Crisp, oval leaves 50-250mm,
from base or spirally arranged
on stem, mostly with toothed
lobes. Flowers June–August.
Yellow, dandelion-like flower-
heads are 20-25mm wide,
each formed by tiny,
hermaphrodite flowers
(florets), within many bracts;
sepals are hair-like; 5 very
unequal petals form a tube;
with 5 stamens and 1 stigma.
Each floret produces a slightly
flattened, 3-ribbed and rough,
nut-like fruit, 2.5-3.5mm long
with a parachute of hairs.
Grows on cultivated or waste
ground.

Daisies

Cat's-ear *Hypochoeris radicata*
From a leafy rosette, this
perennial sends up nearly
leafless flowering stems
20-60cm tall, which exude
milky sap if cut. Leaves
70-250mm, oblong or spear-
shaped, with wavy lobes or
teeth. Flowers June–
September. Bright yellow,
dandelion-like flower-heads
25-40mm wide consist of strap-
shaped, hermaphrodite
flowers (florets), enclosed by
bristly bracts; sepals are hair-
like; 5 very unequal petals
form a tube; with 5 stamens
and 1 stigma. Each floret
produces a ribbed, nut-like
fruit, 4-8mm long, with a
feathery parachute. Grows in
grassland, roadsides, dunes
and lawns.

Beaked Hawk's-beard *Crepis
vesicaria* A bristly biennial or
perennial 10-150cm tall, the
upright, grooved stems
exuding milky sap if cut.
Leaves 100-350mm, from base
or spirally arranged on stem,
spear-shaped, lobed. Flowers
May–July. Loose clusters of
golden yellow, dandelion-like
flower-heads, 15-25mm wide,
each consist of strap-shaped,
hermaphrodite flowers
(florets), enclosed by bristly
bracts; sepals are hair-like; 5
very unequal petals form a
tube; with 5 stamens and 1
stigma. Roughly ribbed, nut-
like fruits are 4-5mm long,
with a hairy, white parachute.
Grows along roads and
railways, on walls or waste
places.

Goat's-beard *Tragopogon pratensis* An annual or perennial with upright stems 30-70cm tall, exuding milky sap if cut. Grass-like, pointed leaves 100-300mm, from base or spirally arranged on stem, each leaf with whitish veins. Flowers June–July. Yellow, solitary, dandelion-like flower-heads 15-22mm long consist of strap-shaped hermaphrodite flowers (florets) surrounded by bracts 25-30mm long; sepals form a ring of hairs; 5 unequal petals form a tube below; with 5 stamens and 1 stigma on a long style. Like a huge, grey dandelion-clock, the fruiting head has fruits 10-22mm long, with feathery parachutes. Grows in grassy places, on waste ground or dunes.

Common Dandelion *Taraxacum officinale* Familiar as a weed or colouring pasture golden yellow, this perennial forms a tuft of leaves, with smooth flowering stems 5-40cm tall exuding milky sap if cut. Leaves 50-400mm, oblong or spear-shaped, lobed and toothed. Flowers March–October. Broad, solitary flower-heads 30-60mm wide consist of yellow, strap-shaped, hermaphrodite flowers (florets), enclosed by bracts 12-25mm long; sepals are hair-like; 5 very unequal petals form a tube; with 5 stamens and 1 stigma. Dandelion-clocks are formed by cylindrical fruits 3.5-4mm long, each with a parachute of hairs. Grows in grassy places and on waste ground.

Water-plantain *Alisma plantago-aquatica* This waterside perennial forms a leafy tuft with upright flowering stems 20-100cm tall. Submerged or floating leaves have a slender blade; most leaves 80-200mm, with an oval or spear-shaped, pointed blade. Flowers June–August. Flowers 8-10mm, hermaphrodite, form a head with branches in rings, pale lilac or white flowers open only in afternoon; the three outer segments of the perianth are oblong, the inner three rounded; with many stamens and stigmas. About 20 dry, oval, flattened fruits form a compact head, each fruit 3-4mm. Grows on edges of ponds, slow rivers or canals.

Bog Asphodel *Narthecium ossifragum* This attractive perennial produces sword-like leaves and upright flowering stems, 5-40cm tall, from a creeping, fleshy main stem. Leaves 50-300mm, slender, pointed, with 5 parallel veins. Flowers July–September. Flowers 12-16mm, hermaphrodite, form a spike 20-100mm long, yellow when open, may turn orange; 6 spreading perianth segments 6-8mm, spear-shaped and equal; with 6 red or orange, woolly stamens and 1 stigma. The tapered, grooved capsule is 10-14mm long, splitting into three to release numerous very slender seeds, each 8-10mm. Grows in bogs, on heaths or moors.

Bluebell *Hyacinthoides non-scripta*
Carpeting woodland floor
with blue, this bulbous
perennial forms a leafy tuft
with arching, leafless
flowering stems 20-50cm tall.
Narrow leaves 20-450mm,
straight-sided with parallel
veins. Flowers April–June.
Flowers 15-20mm,
hermaphrodite, in nodding,
one-sided spikes of 4-16 violet
blue, bell-shaped flowers; 6
parts to perianth are each
15-20mm, joined at the base
and curved back at the tip;
with 6 stamens and 1 stigma.
Fruit 10-15mm, an almost
globular capsule, splits to
release several blackish seeds,
each 3-4mm. Grows in woods,
hedges and on sea-cliffs.
Absent from the north.

Ramsons *Allium ursinum*
Carpets woodland floor but
most noticeable by powerful
aroma of garlic; this bulbous
perennial grows from a leafy
tuft with leafless, upright
flowering stems 10-45cm tall.
Leaves 100-250mm, elliptical,
pointed, with parallel veins.
Flowers April–June. Flowers
16-20mm, hermaphrodite, in
compact, rounded flower-head
of 6-20 white flowers; 6 equal
perianth parts are spear-
shaped and pointed; with 6
stamens and 1 stigma. The
fruit is a deeply 3-lobed
capsule, 8-12mm long, splitting
open to release a few angular,
black seeds, each 3-4mm.
Grows in woods and hedges.

Yellow Iris *Iris pseudacorus* This perennial sends up leafy flowering stems 40-150cm tall from a thick, horizontal stem. Leaves 120-900mm, sword-shaped, in clumps. Flowers May–July. Each flower 80-100mm, hermaphrodite, few flowers cluster near tip of stem; 6 parts of perianth are unequal; the outer three broad and turning downwards, yellow often blotched or spotted with orange and purple; the inner three are yellow, slender and upright; with 3 stamens and 3 huge petal-like stigmas over the outer petals. The oblong, 3-angled capsule is 40-80mm, splitting to release many angular, brown seeds, each 7-9mm long. Grows on edges of rivers and streams, in marshes or woods.

Lords-and-Ladies *Arum maculatum* In spring, the dark green tufts of glossy, often blackish-spotted leaves and leafless, upright flowering stems of this perennial reach 30-50cm tall. Triangular or arrow-shaped leaves are 70-200mm. Flowers April–May. Curious hooded flowers with yellowish-green petal-like bract 150-250mm long, enclosing a flower-spike, upper part smooth, purplish and sterile, lower part with separate male and female flowers, each 1-2.5mm long; no sepals or petals; with 3-4 stamens or 1 stigma. Glossy scarlet berries, 4-6mm long, form elongated clusters, each with 1-3 seeds 3-5mm long. Grows in woods and hedges.

Common Twayblade *Listera ovata* One of the commoner woodland orchids, this perennial has leafy stems 20-60cm tall. A pair of elliptical leaves is most obvious feature of plant, each leaf 50-200mm with 3-5 parallel veins. Flowers June–July. Slender flower-spikes grow 70-250mm long, each of the faintly scented, yellowish-green flowers 14-20mm, hermaphrodite; 3 sepals are oval; 3 petals very unequal, oblong, the large lower petal bent downwards and forked at tip; with 1 stamen and 2 joined stigmas. An almost globular capsule 10mm long, the fruit splits to release myriads of dust-like seeds. Grows in woods, hedges and shady, grassy places.

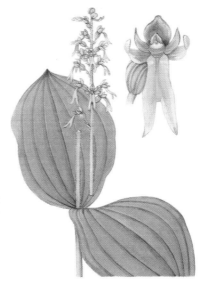

Greater Butterfly-orchid *Platanthera chlorantha* This pale woodland beauty is a perennial, with upright, leafy stems 20-40cm tall. Elliptical leaves arranged spirally on stem, two leaves up to 150mm, with smaller leaves above. With a distinctive scent, greenish-white flowers form a spike 50-200mm long, each flower 18-23mm, hermaphrodite; 3 petal-like sepals are oval to triangular; 3 petals very unequal, side petals spear-shaped, long, narrow lower petal with a spur 19-28mm long; with 1 stamen and 2 stigmas. The oblong, angular capsule splits to release clouds of dust-like seeds. Flowers May–July. Grows in woods and grassy places.

Orchids

Common Spotted-orchid
Dactylorhiza fuchsii Stout,
upright stems of this bulbous
perennial grow 15-70cm tall. A
few elliptical or oval leaves
sheath lower part of stem and
have purplish spots; upper
leaves are scale-like. Flowers
June–August. Flowers
15-20mm, hermaphrodite, pink
or white with reddish spots
and stripes, in a spike; 3 oval
sepals are petal-like; 3 unequal
petals, 2 oval and angled
upwards, large lower petal
deeply 3-lobed with a spur
5.5-6.5mm long; with 1 stamen
and 2 stigmas. Oblong and
angular, the capsule splits to
release numerous, tiny seeds.
Grows in meadows, fens,
marshes and woods.

Early-purple Orchid *Orchis
mascula* One of the commonest
of all orchids in the area, this
bulbous perennial has thick,
upright stems 15-60cm tall.
Leaves spotted purple, oblong
or spear-shaped, 3-5 form a
rosette; upper leaves scale-
like. Flowers April–June.
Reddish-purple flowers form a
spike 40-150mm long, each
hermaphrodite flower
18-26mm long; 3 oval sepals
are petal-like; 3 unequal
petals, 2 oval, large lower
petal 3-lobed with a thick,
blunt spur, 8-11mm long; with
1 stamen and 2 stigmas. The
oblong, angular capsule, splits
to release masses of dust-like
seeds. Grows in grassy places,
woods and hedges.

Further Reading

Clapham, A.R., Tutin, T.G. and Moore, D.M., *Flora of the British Isles*, third edition. Cambridge University Press, Cambridge, 1987.

Clapham, A.R., Tutin, T.G. and Warburg, E.F., *Excursion Flora of the British Isles*, third edition, reprinted with corrections. Cambridge University Press, Cambridge, 1985.

Dony, J.G., Jury, S.L. and Perring, F.H., *English Names of Wild Flowers*, second edition. The Botanical Society of the British Isles, London, 1986.

Fitter, R., Fitter, A. and Blamey, M., *The Wild Flowers of Britain and Northern Europe*, fourth edition. Collins, London, 1986.

Keble Martin, W., *The New Concise British Flora in Colour*. Ebury Press/Michael Joseph, 1982.

Phillips, R., *Wild Flowers of Britain*. Pan, London, 1977.

Polunin, O., *Flowers of Europe: A Field Guide*. Oxford University Press, Oxford, 1969.

Polunin, O., *Collins Photoguide to Wild Flowers of Britain and Northern Europe*. Collins, London, 1988.

Roles, S.J., *Illustrations to the Flora of the British Isles*, vols 1–4. Cambridge University Press, Cambridge, 1957–65.

Ross-Craig, S., *Drawings of British Plants*. G. Bell and Sons, London, 1948–73.

Tutin, T.G., Heywood, V.H., Burges, N.A., Moore, D.M., Valentine, D.H., Walters, S.M. and Webb, D.A. (Eds), *Flora Europaea*, vols 1–5. Cambridge University Press, Cambridge, 1964–80.

Useful Addresses

Botanical Society of the British Isles
c/o The Natural History Museum, Cromwell Road,
London SW7 5BD.

Countryside Council for Wales
Ladywell House, Newtown, Powys SY16 1RD.

English Nature
Northminster House, Peterborough PE1 1UA.

Fauna and Flora Preservation Society
8–12 Camden High Street, London NW1 OJH.

Nature Conservancy Council for Scotland
12 Hope Terrace, Edinburgh EH9 2AS.

Royal Society for Nature Conservation
The Green, Nettleham, Lincs LN2 2NR.

Wild Flower Society
Administrative Office, 68 Outwoods Road,
Loughborough, Leics LE11 3LY.

Index

Index

Index